ROBERT'S RULES OF ORDER IN ACTION

ROBERT'S RULES OF ORDER IN ACTION

How to Participate in Meetings with Confidence

BY RANDI MINETOR

ZEPHYROS
PRESS

DID YOU KNOW?

Brigadier General Henry Martyn Robert III, a US Army engineer, was **inspired** to write his book after he was asked to preside over a public **meeting at his church**. He did the job **so poorly** that he decided to learn parliamentary procedure.

Robert discovered that **people and regions differed greatly** in their interpretations of the **rules for running a meeting**. These clashing interpretations often brought meetings to a **standstill**, especially when the participants were originally from different parts of the country.

The full title of Robert's original book is *Pocket Manual of Rules of Order for Deliberative Assemblies*, and the **first edition was published in 1876**. (In this book, when we're talking about the manual, we'll refer to it as *Robert's Rules of Order*. When we're talking about the principles and procedures themselves, we'll refer to them as Robert's Rules of Order, or simply Robert's Rules.)

Since then, **eleven editions** of *Robert's Rules of Order* have been published. (For information about this work's developmental and printing history, see the **Resources** section at the end of this book.)

More than **5.5 million copies** of *Robert's Rules of Order* remain **in print** today.

...further corrections... the Greater Rochester Summer Opera, and the director will hold auditions... production of *The Marriage of Figaro* from August 21 through... **MEMBER:** Did the scenic designer accept our fee offer? **PRESIDENT:** Thank you... **MEMBER:** Any other questions? *(Silence)* **PRESIDENT:** Is there any discussion about the Fundraising Committee's report? **PRODUCTION COMMITTEE CHAIR:** Mr. President... potential sponsors for the summer season... and that the arts are not one of their focus areas. **PRESIDENT:** Miss Johnson... supporters of issues related to children's health and that the arts are not... giving focus... No, I don't. Thank you for the clarification. **PRESIDENT:** Very well. All those in favor of adopting the agenda say, "Aye." ... before we proceed? *(Silence)* **PRESIDENT:** The agenda is approved. *(Members shuffle papers, turn to one another with comments, talk quietly)* Please stand at ease for a moment... I have determined that the figures discussed are indeed correct. I now call this meeting back to order. **CHAIR:** ...strike out the words "fiction and" and insert the words "narrative, journalistic, and memoir" before the word "nonfiction"... the motion will read as follows: "The National Award of Literary Excellence Foundation will establish the Self-Published... memoir nonfiction categories." The question is on striking out the words "fiction and" and inserting the... the current motion. You may now debate the question. **PRESIDENT:** Thank you, Production Committee. Is there any discussion about the Fundraising Committee's report?... **PRESIDENT:** Very well. Did everyone receive the minutes? **MEMBER:** Yes, I have a correction, with an *m*, not Dumworth, with an *n*. **SECRETARY:** So noted. **PRESIDENT:** Proceed. **MEMBER:** ...the minutes are approved. **PRESIDENT:** The Greater Rochester Summer Opera is on schedule for its production of *A Little Night Music*, to open on... auditions in New York City on March 5, 6, and 7. We are also... **PRESIDENT:** Are there any other questions? *(Around the table, nods and murmurs of assent)*...

CONTENTS

PRESIDENT: Is there any discussion about the summer season. PRODUCTION COMMITTEE CHAIR: Mr. President, we approached potential sponsors for the summer season. Supporters of issues related to children's health and that the arts are not one of their focus areas. Unless my members have further corrections, the Greater Rochester Summer Opera designers, and the director will hold auditions of The Marriage of Figaro from August 21 through...

MEMBER: Did the scenic designer accept our fee offer? PRESIDENT: Any other questions? (Silence) PRESIDENT: You all have in front of you the agenda for today's meeting. Is there any discussion about adopting the agenda? Very well. All those in favor of adopting the agenda say, "Aye."

No, I don't. PRESIDENT: The agenda is approved. Will the secretary read the minutes of the last meeting? before we proceed? (Silence) PRESIDENT: The agenda is approved. Please stand at ease. (Members shuffle papers, turn to one another with comments, talk quietly) PRESIDENT: It has determined that the figures discussed are indeed correct. I now call this meeting back to order. CHAIR: It has the words "fiction and" and insert the words "narrative, journalistic, and memoir" before the word "nonfiction" in the motion will read as follows: "The National Award of Literary Excellence Foundation will establish the Self-Publish memoir nonfiction categories." The question is on striking out the words "fiction and" and inserting the w the current motion. You may now debate the question. PRESIDENT: Thank you, Production Committee.

PRESIDENT: Is there any discussion about the Fundraising Committee's report? MISS JOHNSON: Mr. Presiden the list of potential sponsors for the summer season. PRODUCTION COMMITTEE CHAIR: Mr. President, we that they are supporters of issues related to children's health and that the arts are not one of their focus area (The room quiets) Mr. Secretary, please read the minutes? (Around the table, nods and murmurs of assent) PRESIDENT: Very well. Did everyone receive the minutes? PRESIDENT: Proceed. MEMBER: So noted. PRESIDENT: Are there any minutes? Member: Yes, I have a correction. SECRETARY: May we have the Production Committee's repo Dunworth, with an n, not Dunworth, with an m. SECRETARY: May we have the production of A Little Night Music, to open on A are no further corrections, the minutes are approved. PRESIDENT: its production of A Little Night Music, to open on A R: The Greater Rochester Summer Opera is on schedule for auditions in New York City on March 5, 6, and 7. We are also con d lighting designers, and the director will hold auditions in New York City on March 5, 6, and 7. We are also con roduction of The Marriage of Figaro from August 21 through August 28, and the director will hold auditions bet ke questions. MEMBER: Did the scenic designer accept our fee offer? PRESIDENT: Thank you, Production Committee. Let's move on RESIDENT: Any other questions? (Silence) PRESIDENT: Let's move on ENT: Is there any discussion about the Fundraising Committee's report? MISS JOHNSON: Mr. President, we appr otential sponsors for the summer season. PRODUCTION COMMITTEE CHAIR: Mr. President, we approached supporters of issues related to children's health and that the arts are not one of their focus areas. PRESIDENT: Miss Johnson 's giving focus, I suggest that we not use our limited time to approach them again. PRESIDENT: You all have in front of you the agenda for to NSON: No, I don't. PRESIDENT: The agenda is approved. Will the secretary read the minutes of the last meeting? enda before we proceed? (Silence) PRESIDENT: The agenda is approved. CHAIR (Silence) PRESIDENT: Please stand at ease. (Members shuffle papers, turn to one another with comments, tal er for a moment. Please stand at ease. (Members are indeed correct. I now call this meeting back to order. CH rer and I have determined that the figures discussed are indeed correct. I now call this meeting back to order. CH rike out the words "fiction and" and insert the words "narrative, journalistic, and memoir" before the word "nonfi dopted, the motion will read as follows: "The National Award of Literary Excellence Foundation will establish rnalistic, and memoir nonfiction categories." The question is on striking out the words "fiction and" and inserting to the current motion. You may now debate the question. PRESIDENT: Thank you, Production Committee. Let's PRESIDENT: Is there any discussion about the Fundraising Committee's report? MISS JOHNSON: Mr. President ential sponsors for the summer season. PRODUCTION COMMITTEE CHAIR: Mr. President, we approached supporters of issues related to children's health and that the arts are not one of their focus areas. PRESIDENT: and we were told that they are supporters of issues related to children's health (The room quiets) Mr. Secretary, please read the minutes? (to order. PRESIDENT: Very well. Did everyone receive the minutes? PRESIDENT: S Member: Yes, I have a correction. SECRETARY: with an n, not Dunworth, with an m. SEC the minutes are approved. PRES Opera is on schedule auditions in N

CHAPTER ONE

STRUCTURE
Why We Use Robert's Rules of Order

Whenever people come together in a group to determine a course of action, the members of the group need to discuss the options before them and reach a decision. Not surprisingly, group members rarely find themselves in unanimous agreement about the action to be taken, so they need a way to resolve their differences and move forward, usually by taking some sort of **VOTE**. Such a group is known as a deliberative **ASSEMBLY**. (Throughout this book, the first time we use a term that's defined in the book's glossary, you'll see the term in bold type.)

If you've ever had the misfortune of attending a meeting that went wrong, then you don't need to have the reasons for using Robert's Rules of Order explained to you. Perhaps the meeting's leader had trouble keeping the discussion on track, or the participants kept interrupting one another. Maybe one small faction got hung up on some detail and refused to allow the leader to move through the official **AGENDA**. You may have become frustrated by people talking out of turn, changing the subject, or starting arguments. All in all, it became impossible for the group to accomplish anything.

A deliberative assembly can be as small as a gathering of three people or as large as the US Congress. In any assembly, Robert's Rules of Order can be relied on to establish a baseline of decorum, as well as a process for bringing issues to the **FLOOR**, holding debate, and coming to a vote. Robert's Rules set out not only the basic principles involved in holding and running a productive meeting, but also the procedures that allow group members to make decisions and move forward. These principles and procedures let every member of the group be heard, propose ideas, and have his or her ideas and input treated fairly and respectfully. They also establish procedures for selecting leaders, determining the size of a **MAJORITY**, and protecting the rights of the minority.

Some organizational leaders may fear that using parliamentary procedure to run meetings will look pretentious, or they may believe that a small meeting doesn't require this level of formality. If there are only a few people in a group, using formal rules may seem like a waste of time at first, since it seems reasonable to expect conversation to be more than enough for people to make intelligent decisions.

Even in a small group, however, ground rules allow meetings to be more productive, and they keep the members on track as they go through their decision-making process. The members of a group need to be able to trust that someone is in charge, that a vote will eventually be taken when a **MOTION** is proposed, that the vote will be conducted fairly, that its results will be tallied accurately, and that there are rules determining what the group will do next. And as a group becomes larger—as it grows from, say, three or four people to eight or ten—structure becomes even more important. No group or organization, whether a family or a village council, is too small to use Robert's Rules of Order, and no group decision is so unimportant that it should be made without an orderly vote by its members.

In the pages that follow, you will learn how to become an active and helpful participant in a properly run meeting. Using Robert's Rules, you will discover the proper way to make a proposal, engage in debate, call for and conduct a vote, prepare and make a **REPORT**, make changes to an established decision, and perform the other tasks, large and small, on which orderly meetings depend. Whether you sit on a national nonprofit's board of directors or belong to a local homeowners' or condominium association, you'll learn how to conduct yourself in a manner that allows decisions to be made and plans to be carried out—and people will thank you for your efforts.

ORIGINS AND USES OF ROBERT'S RULES

Brigadier General Henry Martyn Robert III, the creator of Robert's Rules, based them on **PARLIAMENTARY PROCEDURE**, the methods for running a meeting used by the British Parliament, which in turn were derived from the system that was used by the assembly in ancient Greece. In 1876, when General Robert wrote the first edition of his book, he could not have imagined a world where meetings and votes are conducted with participants scattered all over the globe. But many organizations now operate this way, especially professional associations and corporations whose shareholders live thousands of miles from where meetings take place.

Although a far-flung modern assembly can modify Robert's Rules to fit the realities of doing business in the twenty-first century, the rules remain timeless in their ability to help people from different backgrounds, geographical regions, cultures, and levels of experience become productive contributors to group decision-making processes anywhere in the world. That's because virtually anyone, even a total novice, can understand Robert's Rules and put them to good use. Parliamentary procedure may seem austere and mysterious, but Robert's Rules make it simpler than people generally imagine. Any democratically run group or organization that adopts Robert's Rules of Order will find that the rules serve just as well in times of harmony as they do in times of conflict.

We've already discussed some of the kinds of groups, organizations, and gatherings that make Robert's Rules the basis of their meetings. These include boards of directors in the public and private sectors, as well as corporate shareholders, members of homeowners' and condo associations, professional associations, and groups of family members. Here are some other examples:

- Assemblies and committees at all levels of government
- Groups of tribal leaders
- Members of labor unions
- Residents of retirement communities
- Social clubs
- Garden clubs and other hobby-oriented organizations

- Cast and crew members of theatrical productions
- Business coworkers
- Fraternities and sororities
- Adult fraternal and service organizations
- Student-interest organizations
- Groups of school and university classmates and alumni
- Parent-teacher associations
- Employee associations
- Religious groups
- Award-making committees
- Children's community organizations

Just like modern multinational corporations and professional associations, other types of organizations may modify Robert's Rules of Order after adopting the rules as a foundation. A homeowners' association, for example, may have its own governing document that covers the specific rules for the association and its methods of interacting with residents. Such a document usually includes regulations, **BYLAWS**, and restrictions on what residents can do on and with their own property. In addition, the association's voting process may differ significantly from the one in Robert's Rules in that the right to vote may be given, not to the individual resident, but to the lot or property on which the resident lives, which means that each household can vote once as a body. (If you are already a member of a homeowners' or condominium association or plan to become one, be sure to research the association's rules and gain a clear understanding of how its regulations and decision-making process may affect you.)

Other organizations, including the Freemasons, the Rotary Club, the Elks, and college fraternities or sororities, may carry out particular ceremonies in a specific order, particularly when new members are inducted. As a result, these organizations may need to modify the order of business set out in Robert's Rules.

ROBERT'S RULES AND YOU

Maybe you're looking forward to joining a board of directors, a condo association, or another group that conducts meetings and makes decisions. If so, becoming familiar with Robert's Rules of Order will make you a more effective member. If the group already uses Robert's Rules, you'll discover how the rules keep agenda items moving briskly along so that group members can tackle multiple issues in a single meeting and either resolve them on the spot or **REFER** them to committees. And when conflicts do arise, as they always will, you'll see that the organization has tools in place to manage debate, keep tempers in check, and bring about a successful conclusion.

If you're serving as **CHAIR** of your organization, it's a good idea to use Robert's Rules during every meeting instead of bringing the rules in only when you have a major issue to resolve. If you suddenly invoke Robert's Rules when you already have a conflict on your hands, you may look as if you're executing a power play, a perception that may create mistrust and make a reasonable resolution impossible.

But you don't have to be the chair to find Robert's Rules important and useful. To begin with, instead of having to endure interminable meetings filled with interruptions and side discussions, you'll be able to help the group stay on track and move ahead with the topics at hand.

You'll also know how to bring up the issues you would like to see discussed and then see them through to a vote. You'll know what to expect in meetings and how to prepare for debate, and you'll know what form the debate should take.

In addition, you'll understand what your group's leaders expect of you. If you serve on a committee, for example, you may be asked to take **MINUTES** and then provide them later for a full meeting of the organization, or you may need to present a report and answer questions about the committee's activities. When you know what leaders expect, you can prepare materials properly, anticipate likely questions, and give appropriate answers.

At the very least, your familiarity with Robert's Rules will keep you from becoming an obstacle to progress. Sometimes knowing what *not* to do can be just as helpful as knowing the rules for action. When you know how to work within the system and can recognize the right times to speak, act, and debate, you can help make meetings more productive.

further corrections, the Greater Rochester Summer Op... ng designers, and the director will hold aud... n of The Marriage of Figaro from August 21 through... s. MEMBER: Did the scenic designer accept our fee offer? PRESIDENT: Any other questions? (Silence) PRESIDENT: Thank you, Pr... T: Is there any discussion about the Fundraising Committee's report? PRODUCTION COMMITTEE CHAIR: Mr. Presi... ential sponsors for the summer season. PRODUCTION COMMITTEE CHAIR: Mr. Presi... supporters of issues related to children's health and that the arts are not one of their focus areas. ... giving focus, I suggest that we not use our limited time to approach them again. PRESIDENT: You all have in front of you the agenda for today's... No, I don't. Thank you for the clarification. PRESIDENT: Very well. All those in favor of adopting the agenda say, "Aye." M... before we proceed? (Silence) PRESIDENT: The agenda is approved. (Members shuffle papers, turn to one another with comments, talk quietly) P... ence) PRESIDENT: Please stand at ease. (Members shuffle papers, turn to one another with comments, talk quietly) ... ment. Please stand at ease. ... e determined that the figures discussed are indeed correct. I now call this meeting back to order. CHAIR: It has... e words "fiction and" and insert the words "narrative, journalistic, and memoir" before the word "nonfiction" in the... e motion will read as follows: "The National Award of Literary Excellence Foundation will establish the Self-Publis... d memoir nonfiction categories." The question is on striking out the words "fiction and" and inserting the... the current motion. You may now debate the question. PRESIDENT: Thank you, Production Committee. Let... rt. PRESIDENT: Is there any discussion about the Fundraising Committee's report? MISS JOHNSON: Mr. Presi... o the list of potential sponsors for the summer season. PRODUCTION COMMITTEE CHAIR: Mr. President, w... that they are supporters of issues related to children's health and that the arts are not one of their focus are... er. (The room quiets) Mr. Secretary, please read the minutes? (Around the table, nods and murmurs of assent) ... RESIDENT: Very well. Did everyone receive the minutes? PRESIDENT: Proceed. MEMBER: So noted. PRESIDENT: Are there any oth... minutes? Member: Yes, I have a correction, with an n, not Dumworth, with an m. SECRETARY: May we have the Production Committee's rep... Dunworth, with an n, not Dumworth, the minutes are approved. PRESIDENT: for its production of A Little Night Music, to open on... are no further corrections, the minutes are approved. PRESIDENT: auditions in New York City on March 5, 6, and 7. We are also... B: The Greater Rochester Summer Opera is on schedule for its production of A Little Night Music, to open on... d lighting designers, and the director will hold auditions in New York City on March 5, 6, and 7. We are also... production of The Marriage of Figaro from August 21 through August 28, and the director will hold auditions bet... ke questions. MEMBER: Did the scenic designer accept our fee offer? Production Committee Chair: Yes, and he w... PRESIDENT: Any other questions? (Silence) PRESIDENT: Thank you, Production Committee. Let's move on... DENT: Is there any discussion about the Fundraising Committee's report? MISS JOHNSON: Mr. President, we approached... potential sponsors for the summer season. PRODUCTION COMMITTEE CHAIR: Mr. President, we app... supporters of issues related to children's health and that the arts are not one of their focus areas. PROD... n's giving focus, I suggest that we not use our limited time to approach them again. PRESIDENT: You all have in front of you the agenda for to... NSON: No, I don't. Thank you for the clarification. PRESIDENT: Very well. All those in favor of adopting the agenda say, "A... d? (Silence) PRESIDENT: The agenda is approved. (Members shuffle papers, turn to one another with comments, ta... er for a moment. Please stand at ease. (Members shuffle papers, turn to one another with comments, talk quietly) ... rer and I have determined that the figures discussed are indeed correct. I now call this meeting back to order. CH... strike out the words "fiction and" and insert the words "narrative, journalistic, and memoir" before the word "nonf... adopted, the motion will read as follows: "The National Award of Literary Excellence Foundation will establish the... urnalistic, and memoir nonfiction categories." The question is on striking out the words "fiction and" and inserting... nto the current motion. You may now debate the question. PRESIDENT: Thank you, Production Committee. Let's... SIDENT: Is there any discussion about the Fundraising Committee's report? MISS JOHNSON: Mr. President, we app... tial sponsors for the summer season. PRODUCTION COMMITTEE CHAIR: Mr. President, we are not one of their focus areas. PROD... ues related to children's health and that the arts are supporters of issues related to children's health... and we were told that they are supporters of issues related to children's health... to order. (The room quiets) Very well. Did everyone receive the minutes? PRESIDENT... ? Member: Yes, I have a correction, with an n, not Dumworth, with an m. SE... with an n, not Dumworth, the minutes are approved. PRE... Opera is on schedule... auditions in

CHAPTER TWO

MEETINGS
Taking Care of Business

STARTING A MEETING

A **PRESIDING OFFICER** is a person who runs a meeting (note that every meeting is run by a single individual). This officer is elected by the organization's members, usually for a term of a year or more. The presiding officer may be called the **PRESIDENT** or the chair of the organization. (If circumstances arise in which the organization's members select someone to conduct a single meeting, that person may also be called the chair.)

Calling the Meeting to Order

The presiding officer **CALLS THE MEETING TO ORDER**. He or she does this by going to the front of the room or to the head of the table and declaring, in a voice that all can hear, "The meeting will come to order."

Calling for the Minutes to Be Read

The presiding officer calls for the reading of the minutes, which are the notes taken by the **SECRETARY** at the previous

STARTING A MEETING

The members of the board of directors of the Greater Rochester Summer Opera begin their meeting in the conference room of a local church. The president, seated at the head of a long table, speaks first.

PRESIDENT: The meeting will come to order.

(The room quiets)

Mr. Secretary, please read the minutes of the last meeting.

SECRETARY: The minutes were distributed to the membership by e-mail.

PRESIDENT: Very well. Did everyone receive the minutes?

(Around the table, nods and murmurs of assent)

PRESIDENT: Are there any corrections to the minutes?

MEMBER: Yes, I have a correction.

PRESIDENT: Proceed.

MEMBER: The name of the scenic designer for the production of *A Little Night Music* is Kristen Dunworth, with an *n*, not Dumworth, with an *m*.

SECRETARY: So noted.

PRESIDENT: Are there any other corrections?

(Silence)

PRESIDENT: If there are no further corrections, the minutes are approved.

meeting. Depending on the setting for the meeting and the size of the assembly, the secretary may read the minutes standing or seated. Afterward, the presiding officer asks if anyone in attendance wishes to propose changes (such as additions or corrections) to the minutes as read.

Some organizations distribute the previous meeting's minutes in advance of the meeting to allow the participants to review them. In this case, the presiding officer has the option of waiving the reading of the minutes and simply asking if anyone at the meeting has issues with or changes to the minutes.

If there are changes, the secretary will note these, and the presiding officer can ask if there is any debate about the changes. Changes to the minutes are usually made without debate, so the presiding officer can move on to say, "If there are no further corrections, the minutes are approved."

Calling for Reports

The presiding officer calls for reports from various committees. The list of those committees that report at meetings has already been established, so all the committees that need to report know when they will be asked to do so.

Each committee decides on the content of its own report. For example, a report may simply contain information about the committee's activities. Sometimes a committee brings up an issue or proposed action that requires a decision from the assembly. In this case, the presiding officer can call for a motion (**see chapter 3**) and for discussion of the issue and then either refer the issue back to committee or bring it to a vote.

CALLING FOR REPORTS

PRESIDENT: May we have the Production Committee's report, please?

PRODUCTION COMMITTEE CHAIR: The Greater Rochester Summer Opera is on schedule for its production of *A Little Night Music*, to open on August 3. We have hired the scenic, costume, and lighting designers, and the director will hold auditions in New York City on March 5, 6, and 7. We are also completing the contracts for the designers for our production of *The Marriage of Figaro* from August 21 through August 28, and the director will hold auditions between March 23 and March 25. I'll be happy to take questions.

MEMBER: Did the scenic designer accept our fee offer?

PRODUCTION COMMITTEE CHAIR: Yes, and he was grateful for the small increase over last year.

PRESIDENT: Any other questions?

(Silence)

PRESIDENT: Thank you, Production Committee. Let's move on to the Fundraising Committee's report.

Establishing the Presence of a Quorum

It would be wonderful if every member of an organization could come to every meeting and be involved in making every decision. This is unrealistic, however, as most boards of directors and membership organizations are certainly aware. In some cases, only a small group of people can come to a meeting, and the assembly is left without the minimum number of voting members who must be present before a vote can be taken on a motion that has been made or an issue that has been raised.

The number of voting members required to be in attendance before a vote can be taken is called a **QUORUM**. The requirement for a quorum protects the organization from being bound by a vote that was taken when not enough voting members were represented at the meeting.

A quorum is usually a **SIMPLE MAJORITY,** or half the voting members plus one. But every organization considers its own need to have as many members as possible represented and decides for itself how many people will be required for a quorum.

Sometimes a meeting begins with a quorum present, but people need to leave before the meeting ends. This may mean that once an issue under discussion finally comes up for a vote, there's no longer a quorum in the room. If so, any vote the assembly takes will be invalid.

Without a quorum, the assembly can't make any major decisions beyond determining the time and place for the next meeting. That's why there's no good reason to continue a meeting if you don't have a quorum. Even if the members in attendance have a discussion, it will just need to be repeated at the next meeting where a quorum is present so that the members can be fully updated before a vote. A discussion is considered to be **SUBSTANTIVE BUSINESS**, which means that a quorum has to be in attendance.

OBSERVING DECORUM

How should you behave in a meeting? Throughout its pages, *Robert's Rules of Order* lays out basic principles for debate and other forms of discourse, but let's bring them together here to clarify what is appropriate:

OBSERVING DECORUM

PRESIDENT: Is there any discussion about the Fundraising Committee's report?

MISS JOHNSON: Mr. President, I suggest that we add Xoron Corporation to the list of potential sponsors for the summer season.

PRODUCTION COMMITTEE CHAIR: Mr. President, we approached Xoron last year, and we were told that they are supporters of issues related to children's health and that the arts are not one of their focus areas. Unless my colleague has any new information about Xoron's giving focus, I suggest that we not use our limited time to approach them again.

PRESIDENT: Miss Johnson, do you have any new information?

MISS JOHNSON: No, I don't. Thank you for the clarification.

- **ARRIVE ON TIME.** When the appointed hour arrives, be ready to begin.

- **KEEP CROSS TALK TO A MINIMUM.** To ask a question or make a comment, raise your hand and wait until the presiding officer calls on you.

- **DON'T TALK OR WHISPER WHILE OTHERS ARE TALKING.** Observe the same restraint when it comes to walking around the room or getting coffee during a meeting. Some organizations don't object to this kind of behavior, but it can be as disruptive as whispering. Give people the respect you hope they will give you.

- **DON'T ENGAGE IN PERSONAL ATTACKS.** In any discussion, do not make accusations or negative comments about anyone on the other side of an issue. It is appropriate to say, "I respectfully disagree with my colleague." It is inappropriate to say, "Bob is lying about that."

- **STICK TO THE SUBJECT.** Long tangents and irrelevant information will not help you make your point. Talk about the issue at hand, and save other topics for later discussions.

- **ADDRESS THE CHAIR.** The best way to avoid attacking someone or being attacked yourself is to make all your statements to the presiding officer rather than directly to your colleagues. Say, for example, "Mr. President, could the secretary please read the last part of the minutes again?" Don't address the secretary by saying, "Michael, you got that completely wrong. Read it again."

- **TURN OFF YOUR MOBILE PHONE.** Obviously, this isn't one of the original Robert's Rules, but the principles of decorum should certainly include keeping device-related interruptions to an absolute minimum.

- **FOLLOW THE BEST EXAMPLE.** The fact that others are breaking the rules should not be seen as permission for you to do so.

ESTABLISHING A STANDARD ORDER OF BUSINESS

Most organizations establish a **STANDARD ORDER OF BUSINESS** for their meetings. It specifies the order in which members will give reports, address **UNFINISHED BUSINESS**, and take on new business. A standard order of business makes meetings predictable, helps members prepare and present information, and keeps things moving along.

Here is the standard order of business according to Robert's Rules:

- **APPROVAL OF THE AGENDA.** An agenda is different from a standard order of business in that it may include things that are not elements of the standard order, such as a ceremony, a lunch break, a **RECESS**, or a special program. The agenda may also specify time limits and durations for particular agenda items. If an organization chooses to use an agenda, as most small organizations do, the assembly must approve and adopt it at the beginning of the meeting. Usually, that takes only a moment, and then the assembly can proceed with its business.

APPROVING THE AGENDA

PRESIDENT: You all have in front of you the agenda for today's meeting. Are there any additions to the agenda before we proceed?

(Silence)

PRESIDENT: Very well. All those in favor of adopting the agenda say, "Aye."

MEMBERS: Aye.

PRESIDENT: Any opposed?

(Silence)

PRESIDENT: The agenda is approved. Will the secretary read the minutes of the last meeting?

- **READING AND APPROVAL OF THE PREVIOUS MEETING'S MINUTES.** Agreement on what happened at the previous meeting can be key to proceeding with the organization's business, not only at the next meeting, but also throughout the organization. Some members may not see the minutes as particularly important, but a meeting's minutes stand as the legal record of the organization's activity and decisions. Should a court proceeding ever be brought against the organization, the minutes will provide evidence of what did and did not happen at a particular meeting. This procedural step should be treated with the care it deserves.

- **OFFICERS' AND STANDING COMMITTEES' REPORTS ON THEIR ACTIVITY.** Well before the meeting, the person who creates the agenda should contact the officers and the standing committee chairs to determine whether they have reports to present. If they don't—for example, if a committee has not met since presenting its last report—then they are not required to give reports unless the organization's bylaws say that they must. When reports are given at the meeting, members have the opportunity to ask questions and discuss the issues that the committees have brought forward.

- **REPORTS BY SPECIAL COMMITTEES.** If an organization has special committees, they present their reports after the standing committees have presented theirs. Again, the members in attendance can ask questions, discuss issues, and determine whether any decisions that require a vote need to be made.

- **PRESENTATION OF SPECIAL ORDERS.** These are high-priority agenda items. For example, if a meeting is held at the time of year when members elect the organization's officers, then that vote will be taken at this point in the agenda. This is also the time for special items, if any, that require a two-thirds majority vote (**see chapter 8**). If there are no special orders, then there's no need to place this item on the agenda.

- **DISCUSSION OF UNFINISHED BUSINESS.** Many organizations erroneously call this old business, but **OLD BUSINESS**, by definition, has already been completed at previous meetings. **UNFINISHED BUSINESS**, as the term is correctly used, is business that was still under discussion when the last meeting was adjourned. Unfinished business usually involves a motion that was postponed until the current meeting but was not made a special order (and is therefore known as a general order). Any unfinished business to be discussed at the meeting is listed on the agenda. If there is no unfinished business, then there's no need to place this item on the agenda.

- **DISCUSSION OF NEW BUSINESS.** Any issues that are to be discussed for the first time at the meeting are considered new business. At this point of the meeting, the presiding officer is required to call for new business, and members have the right to bring up issues they want the organization to consider. It isn't necessary to notify the presiding officer of new business that will be brought up at the meeting, but it's a good idea to do this in order to have it placed on the agenda, especially if the issue will lead to lengthy debate.

- **ADJOURNMENT.** The presiding officer draws the meeting to its official close.

PAUSING OR ENDING A MEETING

There are two ways to pause a meeting, and one way to end it:

- **RECESS.** The assembly may decide to take a break, or recess, from the meeting. A majority vote by the members in attendance is required, with a brief discussion about the length of the recess. The group may choose to recess for a specific amount of time—say, 15 minutes—or to recess until called back to order by the chair.

- **CHAIR'S ORDER TO STAND AT EASE.** If an issue arises about which the chair needs to confer with other officers or another member for a few minutes, the chair may order the assembly to **STAND AT EASE**. This means that the members remain in their seats until the chair calls the meeting back to order.

ORDERING THE ASSEMBLY TO STAND AT EASE

PRESIDENT: I need to confer with the treasurer for a moment. Please stand at ease.

(Members shuffle papers, turn to one another with comments, talk quietly)

PRESIDENT: Thank you. The treasurer and I have determined that the figures discussed are indeed correct. I now call this meeting back to order.

- **ADJOURNMENT.** When the assembly has come to the end of the agenda and finished with all its items, the presiding officer ends the meeting by adjourning it.

CHAPTER THREE

MOTIONS
Making a Proposal

Robert's Rules of Order specifies five classes of motions:

1. Main motions
2. Subsidiary motions
3. Privileged motions
4. Incidental motions
5. Motions that bring a question back before the assembly

Main motions, as their name implies, are considered primary motions. Subsidiary, privileged, and incidental motions are considered secondary motions, which means that they're used to help the assembly determine the best way to handle a main motion (for example, when questions arise about the organization's rules or about how to make a debate productive and keep the organization's business moving efficiently at the current meeting). This chapter looks at all five types of motions and how they apply to the business of an organization.

MAIN MOTIONS

MOTIONS

If your organization uses Robert's Rules, and if you attend a meeting where one or more decisions have to be reached, you will have at least one opportunity to make a motion, which is an official proposal that the members in attendance take some type of action. A motion can be about any kind of business, including the election of new officers; a decision about how the organization's money will be spent; and the possibility of taking on a new project, scheduling a special event, or enacting a piece of legislation.

We'll discuss the procedures for debate in chapter 4. For now, let's establish that there can be no debate about an issue until someone has made a **MAIN MOTION**, which is a call to introduce a piece of business for the first time. When a main motion is on the floor, that piece of business is the only one that the assembly can discuss. The group must resolve this motion in one way or another before moving on to the next piece of business.

Here is the process for making a motion:

- **A PARTICIPANT STANDS UP (OR, IN A SMALL MEETING, RAISES HIS OR HER HAND) AND ADDRESSES THE PRESIDING OFFICER, OR CHAIR.** This indicates to the chair that the participant wishes to speak. For example, the participant stands and says, "Madam President" or "Mr. Chairman." The person who proposes a motion is called a **MOVER**.

- **THE CHAIR INDICATES THAT THE MOVER MAY SPEAK.** The chair may address the mover by name—"Ms. Jones," for example, or "Mr. Green"—or, at a small meeting, the chair may simply say, "Yes" and nod to the mover. The chair may

MAKING AND SECONDING A MOTION

The members of the board of directors of the Girl Scouts of Pennington County hold their monthly meeting to plan activities and deal with administrative issues.

MS. JONES: Madam President.

(Ms. Jones rises)

PRESIDENT: Ms. Jones, you have the floor.

MS. JONES: I move that the Girl Scouts of Pennington County add a field trip to Custer State Park to our calendar for next fall.

(Ms. Jones takes her seat)

MRS. ORWELL: Second!

PRESIDENT: Ms. Jones, to clarify, do you mean the fall of 2016?

MS. JONES: I do.

PRESIDENT: A motion is made and seconded that the Girl Scouts of Pennington County add a field trip to Custer State Park to our calendar for the fall of 2016.

add, "You have the floor." This means that the mover is authorized to speak.

- **THE MOVER IMMEDIATELY PROPOSES THE MOTION.**
  He or she begins by saying, "I move that we ... " (here, the mover informs the assembly about the proposal). For example, the mover may say, "I move that the Girl Scouts of Pennington County add a field trip to Custer State Park to our calendar for the fall of next year." It is important to be

very specific in proposing a motion. The words of the motion will go into the minutes exactly as spoken. If the assembly votes in favor of the proposal, it becomes law for the organization, so the motion should not be left open to any interpretation that could be used later to controvert its meaning. Some presiding officers require a main motion to be submitted in writing. This practice ensures that the motion is entered into the minutes and considered by the assembly exactly as written. Even if a chair does not require this formality, it's a good idea to write a motion out and read its words when the motion is presented to the assembly.

- **AFTER PROPOSING THE MOTION, THE MOVER SITS DOWN.** This is not the time for the mover to tell the assembly why the motion deserves consideration. There will be time later to make that case.

- **SOMEONE SECONDS THE MOTION.** Another member of the assembly must **SECOND** the motion before it can be considered. This person does not have to agree with the motion. A second simply gives the group permission to discuss the motion. The person seconding the motion will either say, "I second the motion" or simply call out, "Second!" The person who seconds the motion may do so while seated and without asking the chair for the floor.

- **THE PRESIDING OFFICER STATES THE QUESTION.** At this point, if there are issues with the way the motion has been stated, the mover and the chair can work through the exact language until it expresses what the mover intended. When the mover agrees with the wording, the presiding officer

states the question: "It is moved and seconded that . . ."
(here, the chair repeats the motion verbatim).

- **THE ASSEMBLY CONSIDERS THE MOTION.** Now that the
motion has been made and the question has been stated for
the assembly, the presiding officer can open the floor to
debate. (The rules of debate are specific and are outlined in
detail in chapter 4.)

SUBSIDIARY MOTIONS

A **SUBSIDIARY MOTION** affects the main motion currently on
the floor. Members of the assembly can propose more than one
subsidiary motion to address various issues that arise before or
during a debate. These different subsidiary motions are assigned
different orders of precedence so that the assembly can address
them one at a time in a specific order. The following subsidiary
motions are listed in descending order of precedence. In other
words, if every one of these subsidiary motions were to be proposed, the assembly would deal first with the motion at the top
of the list:

- **MOTION TO LAY THE MAIN MOTION ON THE TABLE.** This
motion temporarily sets the main motion aside. When the
assembly agrees to set the main motion aside in this way, the
members are said to **TABLE** the motion. This motion may be
used if there is another topic to be discussed that will have
an impact on the current topic under discussion.

- **MOTION TO CALL FOR THE PREVIOUS QUESTION.** The
motion to call for the **PREVIOUS QUESTION** stops debate on
the main motion. This motion may be used to end a debate

LAYING A MOTION ON THE TABLE

MRS. SMITH: Madam President.

(Mrs. Smith rises)

PRESIDENT: Mrs. Smith, you have the floor.

MRS. SMITH: I move that we lay the motion to add a field trip to Custer State Park in 2016 on the table until we hear the treasurer's report and determine whether the trip is affordable.

(Mrs. Smith takes her seat)

MISS MASON: Second!

PRESIDENT: A motion has been made and seconded to lay the main motion on the table. Is there any discussion?

that has become contentious, or one in which the argument is not progressing in a constructive way.

- **MOTION TO LIMIT DEBATE OR EXTEND THE LIMITS ON DEBATE.** If people on either side of a main motion have not had the opportunity to speak within the time limit set by the chair, a member of the assembly may move to extend the limits of the debate. Likewise, if members know that debate on a particularly controversial issue is likely to go on indefinitely, a member can move to limit the length of the debate.

- **MOTION TO POSTPONE A DEBATE OR A VOTE TO A CERTAIN TIME.** This motion allows the assembly to put off debating or voting on the main motion until another meeting or until information relevant to the motion becomes available.

LIMITING DEBATE

MISS MASON: Madam President, I move that we limit debate on this motion to five minutes per speaker and to three speakers on each side of the issue.

MRS. SMITH: Second!

- **MOTION TO REFER THE MAIN MOTION TO COMMITTEE.** Some main motions require more study or investigation before the assembly can productively consider them. These motions can be referred to one of the organization's standing committees for additional inquiry, or a special committee can be formed to look into them (**see chapter 6**).

- **MOTION TO AMEND THE MAIN MOTION.** If debate on the main motion reveals that it requires some type of adjustment, a member of the assembly can move to amend the motion. It is necessary to determine exactly what the main motion should say before proposing a subsidiary motion to amend it. (For more about amendments, **see chapter 5**.)

- **MOTION TO POSTPONE THE MAIN MOTION INDEFINITELY.** If a main motion is determined to be inappropriate at the current time for any reason, a member of the assembly can move to postpone the motion indefinitely. This effectively kills the motion, although someone may eventually move to resurrect it (see "Motions That Bring a Question Back Before the Assembly," later in this chapter). With the main motion postponed indefinitely, the assembly can move on to other business.

AMENDING A MOTION

MRS. ORWELL: Madam President, I wish to make a motion.

(Mrs. Orwell rises)

PRESIDENT: You have the floor.

MRS. ORWELL: I move that we amend the motion to read as follows: "Troop 266 of the Girl Scouts of Pennington County should add a field trip to Custer State Park to the calendar for the spring of 2017."

(Mrs. Orwell takes her seat)

MS. JONES: Second!

PRESIDENT: A subsidiary motion has been made and seconded to amend the main motion to read as follows: "Troop 266 of the Girl Scouts of Pennington County should add a field trip to Custer State Park to the calendar for the spring of 2017."

PRIVILEGED MOTIONS

A **PRIVILEGED MOTION** becomes an option when the assembly confronts a matter of procedure that must be dealt with right away. Privileged motions have to do with the meeting in general, not with the main motion on the floor, but they take precedence over debate and any other business in progress. These motions are not debated. When a member makes a privileged motion, it must be voted on before the meeting can continue. Once it has been made and seconded, the chair moves immediately to the vote.

- **MOTION TO FIX THE TIME TO WHICH TO ADJOURN.** This is not a motion for the current meeting to come to an end

FIXING THE TIME TO WHICH TO ADJOURN

MRS. SMITH: Madam President, I move that we fix the time to which to adjourn at 3 p.m. on Tuesday, April 28.

MISS MASON: Second!

PRESIDENT: The motion has been made and seconded to fix the time to which to adjourn at 3 p.m. on Tuesday, April 28. All those in favor, please signify by raising your hands.

(even though, in this situation, the meeting may have to be brought to a close—maybe abruptly—for some reason). Instead, it's a motion to continue the business of the current meeting at a later time (for example, because the issue being discussed is too complex for a single meeting). When a member moves to fix the time to which to adjourn, he or she sets a later time and/or date when the current meeting will be continued.

- **MOTION TO ADJOURN.** A motion to adjourn is a fairly standard procedure at the end of any meeting. It brings the meeting to an immediate close.

- **MOTION TO RECESS.** A member can move for a break in the meeting until a specific time. A brief discussion is allowed about the length of the recess and the time at which the group will reconvene. The assembly may choose to recess either for a specific interval or until called again to order by the chair.

- **QUESTION OF PRIVILEGE.** Any issue related to the welfare of the assembly or its individual members can be raised as a

RAISING A QUESTION OF PRIVILEGE

PRESIDENT: Let's move on to the next order of business.

MRS. SMITH: Madam President, I need to raise a question of privilege.

PRESIDENT: Go ahead, Mrs. Smith.

MRS. SMITH: I am having trouble hearing over the street noise coming through the window. Will anyone mind if I close it?

PRESIDENT: Any objections from the assembly?

(Members murmur assent to Mrs. Smith's request)

PRESIDENT: Go ahead and close it, Mrs. Smith.

MRS. SMITH: Thank you.

(Mrs. Smith closes the window)

question of privilege. For example, some members may not be able to hear the discussion because another member is speaking too softly or because the sound system is set too low. The meeting room may be too hot or too cold. A member may suddenly need an ambulance to be called. A bomb threat, a fire alarm, and other safety-related events and issues that require immediate attention can also be raised as questions of privilege.

- **CALL FOR THE ORDERS OF THE DAY.** If the assembly has strayed from the agenda and gone off on a tangent, any member can call for the orders of the day. When this motion is made, the chair needs to return the assembly to the agenda items that constitute the meeting's standard order of business (**see chapter 1**) and get the discussion back on track.

INCIDENTAL MOTIONS

"Incidental," in this case, describes any procedural motion related to something that has occurred during consideration of the business at hand. For example, a member of the assembly may wish to check on the proper rules for handling a specific issue. Whenever someone makes an incidental motion, business stops so that the group can deal immediately with the procedural question. Unlike subsidiary motions, incidental motions are addressed right away, and so they have no order of precedence.

- **POINT OF ORDER.** At any time during a debate or discussion, a member can interrupt the proceedings to raise a point of order, indicating that a rule may have been broken. A point of order calls for the chair to make a ruling before the meeting's business can continue.

- **MOTION TO APPEAL.** A member who disagrees with a ruling by the chair can move to **APPEAL** the chair's decision. This motion usually prompts the chair to listen to the member's reasoning and make a new decision in response. But a chair who still has a sense of being in the right will probably say so and then work to resolve the issue.

- **CALL FOR DIVISION OF THE ASSEMBLY.** A member may doubt the results of the vote on a main motion, especially if the vote was taken by voice. This incidental motion calls for

RAISING A POINT OF ORDER

DR. JENKINS: . . . and this is why I say that we cannot allow our young girls to be placed in danger by exposing them to free-ranging buffalo and burros in Custer State Park. Now, I still have three minutes to speak, so I will read to you from *Scouting for Girls: The Official Handbook of the Girl Scouts*.

MS. JONES: Point of order!

(Ms. Jones rises)

PRESIDENT: The chair recognizes Ms. Jones.

MS. JONES: The rules of debate are clear on this. Dr. Jenkins cannot use her debate time for activities that are not germane to the topic at hand.

(Ms. Jones takes her seat)

PRESIDENT: Agreed. The point of order is sustained. Dr. Jenkins, do you have anything to add to your argument that is relevant to the debate?

DR. JENKINS: No, Madam President.

PRESIDENT: Please be seated. Who would now like to speak in favor of the motion?

a physical division of the assembly, with the members in favor of the main motion going to one part of the room and those opposed going to another. In a smaller group, the call for **DIVISION** can be answered with a standing vote, in which first those in favor of the main motion and then those opposed to it rise and remain standing while they are counted. The chair may appoint **TELLERS** to count the members on each side (**see chapter 8**).

- **REQUEST OR INQUIRY.** A number of motions fall into this category. They include making a request for permission to modify or withdraw a motion, a request to read papers associated with a motion, and a request for any other privilege, among other requests. All such requests stop other business until they are fulfilled. A member who makes an inquiry may want to research a point of information that has been offered in debate or review parliamentary procedure in connection with a specific incident (sometimes a member who actually wants to make an inquiry into a detail of parliamentary procedure makes the mistake of raising a point of order). An inquiry, like a request, stops debate or other proceedings until the inquiry has been completed.

- **MOTION TO SUSPEND THE RULES.** It may seem contrary to the entire basis of Robert's Rules, but sometimes a suspension of parliamentary procedure can be effective. The suspension may be used to pass a noncontroversial bureaucratic motion quickly, without the need for debate. In both houses of the US Congress, for example, a number of rules may be suspended to forestall speeches by senators and representatives. Some rules cannot be suspended, however. For example, the rules that govern the fundamental rights of an assembly or its individual members must be in force at all times.

- **CALL FOR DIVISION OF THE QUESTION.** Sometimes a motion is too complex to pass as a unit, especially if it includes more than one action. For example, a motion proposing that troops 266 and 494 be combined into one

SUSPENDING THE RULES

PRESIDENT: A motion has been made and seconded to combine troops 266 and 494 into one Pennington County Girl Scout troop. We may now debate the question.

MRS. SMITH: Madam President, I move that we suspend the rules and go right to a vote on this motion.

PRESIDENT: Any second?

MRS. MASON: Second!

PRESIDENT: All those in favor of suspending the rules and moving right to a vote, signify by saying, "Aye."

ALMOST ALL MEMBERS: Aye.

PRESIDENT: All those opposed, signify by saying, "No."

TWO MEMBERS: No.

PRESIDENT: The ayes have it, and the rules are suspended. We will now proceed with a vote on the motion to combine troops 266 and 494 into one Pennington County Girl Scout troop. All those in favor, say, "Aye."

ALMOST ALL MEMBERS: Aye.

PRESIDENT: All those opposed, signify by saying, "No."

TWO MEMBERS: No.

PRESIDENT: The ayes have it. The motion to combine troops 266 and 494 into one Pennington County Girl Scout troop is passed.

Pennington County Girl Scout troop and allocating $20,000 to the combined troop for the costs of a field trip and operating expenses until the end of 2019 may put too many things at stake all at once. If debate about the financial allocation threatens to derail the consolidation of the two troops, a member of the assembly may call for division of the question into two separate motions. This incidental motion would allow the question of troop consolidation to be decided separately.

- **OBJECTION TO CONSIDERATION OF A QUESTION.** If a member believes that the assembly should not consider a motion that has already been made and seconded, that member can immediately derail the debate by objecting to consideration of the question, thus forcing the assembly to resolve this incidental motion before continuing the discussion.

MOTIONS THAT BRING A QUESTION BACK BEFORE THE ASSEMBLY

If a member wants the assembly to reconsider a motion that was set aside at a previous meeting, the member must bring that motion back to the floor. A number of different kinds of motions can be used for this purpose. All of them must be made when no other business is pending and when no other motion is on the floor. A previously set-aside motion that is brought back for consideration is regarded as new business.

- **MOTION TO TAKE A MOTION FROM THE TABLE.** This motion is useful when a main motion was temporarily set aside until a missing piece of information could be obtained. It is reasonable for such a previously set-aside main motion to be brought back for consideration.

- **MOTION TO RECONSIDER A VOTE.** If the sense of the assembly is that the members want to change their minds about a vote that has just been taken at the current meeting, a member can move that the assembly reconsider the vote. This motion opens the question up to new debate.

- **MOTION TO RESCIND THE ACTION.** Members of the assembly may decide that they want to reconsider a vote taken either in a meeting that has just adjourned or in an earlier meeting. In this situation, a member can move to rescind the assembly's action, thus bringing the main motion back up for debate before the vote on rescindment.

- **MOTION TO AMEND A PREVIOUSLY ADOPTED MAIN MOTION.** After a meeting has adjourned, the members of the assembly may decide that a main motion that passed is actually flawed and needs to be revisited. At a later meeting, a member can move to make an **AMENDMENT** to the previously approved motion, bringing the question back for debate and a vote on the proposed changes.

- **MOTION TO DISCHARGE A COMMITTEE.** This motion takes a main motion out of committee before the committee in question has made its final recommendation to the assembly.

RECONSIDERING THE VOTE

PRESIDENT: The ayes have it. The motion to combine troops 266 and 494 into one Pennington County Girl Scout troop is passed.

MRS. O'HARA: Madam President, I move that we reconsider the vote.

PRESIDENT: On what grounds?

MRS. O'HARA: With no debate, it did not come to light that the members of troop 494 will have to be driven half an hour each way to attend troop meetings and events. This is excessive, and it will most likely cause many girls to leave the troop.

PRESIDENT: Is there a second?

DR. JENKINS: Second!

PRESIDENT: Very well, a motion has been made and seconded to reconsider the vote on the combination of troops 266 and 494. We will now open this matter for debate.

PRESIDENT: Did the scenic designer accept our fee offer? ... Is there any discussion about the Fundraising Committee's report? PRODUCTION COMMITTEE CHAIR: Mr. President ... Is there any discussion of issues related to children's health and that the arts are not one of their focus areas ... supporters of issues related to children's health and that the arts are not one of their focus areas. PRESIDENT: Miss Johnson ... giving focus, I suggest that we not use our limited time to approach them again. PRESIDENT: You all have in front of you the agenda for today's ... No, I don't. Thank you for the clarification. PRESIDENT: Very well. All those in favor of adopting the agenda say, "Aye." PRESIDE ... before we proceed? (Silence) PRESIDENT: The agenda is approved. Will the secretary read the minutes of the last meeting? PRESID ... ence) PRESIDENT: Please stand at ease. (Members shuffle papers, turn to one another with comments, talk quietly) ... ment. Please stand at ease. (Members shuffle papers, turn to one another with comments, talk quietly) CHAIR: It has ... e determined that the figures discussed are indeed correct. I now call this meeting back to order. CHAIR: It has ... e words "fiction and" and insert the words "narrative, journalistic, and memoir" before the word "nonfiction" in the ... e motion will read as follows: "The National Award of Literary Excellence Foundation will establish the Self-Publish ... and memoir nonfiction categories." The question is on striking out the words "fiction and" and inserting the ... the current motion. You may now debate the question. PRESIDENT: Thank you, Production Committee ... rt. PRESIDENT: Is there any discussion about the Fundraising Committee's report? PRODUCTION COMMITTEE CHAIR: Mr. Presi ... o the list of potential sponsors for the summer season. PRODUCTION COMMITTEE CHAIR: Mr. President, w ... that they are supporters of issues related to children's health and that the arts are not one of their focus are ... r. (The room quiets) Mr. Secretary, please read the minutes? (Around the table, nods and murmurs of assent) ... er. (The room quiets) Mr. Secretary, please read the minutes? (Around the table, nods and murmurs of assent) The minutes ... PRESIDENT: Very well. Did everyone receive the minutes? PRESIDENT: Proceed. MEMBER: The name of the scenic designer for ... inutes? Member: Yes, I have a correction. PRESIDENT: Very well. SECRETARY: The minutes ... Dunworth, with an n, not Dumworth, with an m. SECRETARY: May we have the Production Committee's ... are no further corrections, the minutes are approved. PRESIDENT: So noted. PRESIDENT: Are there any oth ... R: The Greater Rochester Summer Opera is on schedule for its production of A Little Night Music, to open on ... d lighting designers, and the director will hold auditions in New York City on March 5, 6, and 7. We are also co ... production of The Marriage of Figaro from August 21 through August 28, and the director will hold auditions bet ... ke questions. MEMBER: Any other questions? (Silence) PRESIDENT: Thank you, Production Committee. Let's move on ... PRESIDENT: Any other questions? (Silence) PRESIDENT: Thank you, Production Committee. Let's move on ... DENT: Is there any discussion about the Fundraising Committee's report? MISS JOHNSON: Mr. President, I suggg ... potential sponsors of issues related to children's health and that the arts are not one of their focus areas. Unless my ... supporters of issues related to children's health and that the arts are not one of their focus areas. PRESIDENT: Miss Johnso ... n's giving focus, I suggest that we not use our limited time to approach them again. PRESIDENT: Miss Johnso ... NSON: No, I don't. Thank you for the clarification. PRESIDENT: You all have in front of you the agenda for to ... enda before we proceed? (Silence) PRESIDENT: Very well. All those in favor of adopting the agenda say, "A ... ? (Silence) PRESIDENT: The agenda is approved. Will the secretary read the minutes of the last meeting? ... er for a moment. Please stand at ease. (Members shuffle papers, turn to one another with comments, ta ... urer and I have determined that the figures discussed are indeed correct. I now call this meeting back to order. CR ... strike out the words "fiction and" and insert the words "narrative, journalistic, and memoir" before the word "nonf ... adopted, the motion will read as follows: "The National Award of Literary Excellence Foundation will establish ... urnalistic, and memoir nonfiction categories." The question is on striking out the words "fiction and" and inserting ... nto the current motion. You may now debate the question. PRESIDENT: Thank you, Production Committee. Let's ... SIDENT: Is there any discussion about the Fundraising Committee's report? PRODUCTION COMMITTEE CHAIR: Mr. Presiden ... tial sponsors for the summer season, PRODUCTION COMMITTEE CHAIR: Mr. President, we app ... ues related to children's health and that the arts are not one of their focus areas. PROD ... and we were told that they are supporters of issues related to children's health ... to order. (The room quiets) Member: Yes, I have a correction. PRESIDENT: Very well. Did everyone receive the minutes? ... with an n, not Dumworth, with an m. SE ... the minutes are approved. PRE ... Opera is on schedule ... auditions

CHAPTER FOUR

DEBATE
Arguing Your Side

Once a motion has been made and seconded, the chair will open the floor to debate about the motion before it comes to a vote. In this chapter, we'll look at the rules for debate and the methods available to limit or extend debate, as required. We'll also take a closer look at some of the privileged motions discussed in chapter 3 that are not debatable.

RULES FOR DEBATE

- **SPEECH LIMITS.** According to Robert's Rules, each member of the assembly who wishes to speak during the debate on a motion may do so twice a day. The member may speak for up to 10 minutes, although your organization may have special rules for debate that allow more or less time. A member who does not use all 10 minutes each time forfeits the rest of the time; it cannot be transferred or yielded to someone else. (This is different from what you may have observed in the US Congress, where members are allowed

PERMISSION TO SPEAK OUT OF TURN

In spite of the protocol governing who will be called to speak after the previous speaker yields the floor, there are three exceptions under which a member may be called to speak even without having been the first one to stand:

1. **THE MEMBER IS THE ONE WHO MADE THE MOTION THAT IS BEING DEBATED.** The mover has a one-time right to supersede others and speak when he or she chooses. Most movers use this right to be the first speaker when debate begins.

2. **THE MEMBER HAS NOT YET SPOKEN IN THE DEBATE.** When others who rise have already had a chance to speak, the member who has not yet spoken will be given preference.

3. **THE MEMBER IS THE ONLY PERSON WHO RISES TO SPEAK AGAINST THE MOTION, AND SOMEONE HAS JUST SPOKEN IN FAVOR OF IT.** The chair will give the member who opposes the motion the next chance to speak, since the debate should alternate between members who are for the motion and members who are against it.

to yield portions of their time to another member.) If a member of an assembly so chooses, however, he or she may use part of the allotted time to take questions from other members.

- **RECOGNITION BY THE CHAIR.** To be allowed to speak, a member must stand when the person who has just spoken **YIELDS** the floor—that is, when that person finishes speaking and sits down. The chair will (or should) recognize the first person who rises after the previous speaker has concluded. It's important for whoever wants to speak next

BECOMING THE NEXT MEMBER TO SPEAK

The governing council of the City of Underberg takes up the issue of financial support for construction of a new soccer stadium downtown.

MR. RUSSELL: . . . and that's why I believe we should support the construction of a new soccer stadium in downtown Underberg.

(Mr. Russell takes his seat)

DR. WATSON: Mr. Chairman!

(Dr. Watson rises)

MR. HOLMES: Mr. Chairman!

(Mr. Holmes rises)

MRS. WHITE: Mr. Chairman!

(Mrs. White rises)

CHAIR: We've just heard from someone who is for the motion to support the stadium. Which one of you wishes to speak against the motion?

(Mr. Holmes and Mrs. White take their seats)

CHAIR: Dr. Watson, you have the floor for 10 minutes.

DR. WATSON: Thank you, Mr. Chairman. The soccer stadium is too expensive a project for the city of Underberg to take on at this time. I have the city's budget with me today, and . . .

not to rise until the previous person has yielded. Doing otherwise can cost a member the opportunity to be the next one to speak. A member who rises to speak should simultaneously call out the title of the chair.

- **SPEAK ON THE SUBJECT.** Each member's remarks must be **GERMANE** to the topic at hand. In other words, they must be about the motion on the floor. No member may get up and read the phone book or tell a long story that is not relevant to the motion, although a member may present evidence that supports the case for or against the motion.

- **AVOID PERSONAL ATTACKS.** Debate is about issues, not about how much the members of the assembly like or dislike the people they're debating. If a member has issues with an opponent's point of view, the member must criticize what appears to be the thinking behind that point of view or the

AVOIDING PERSONAL ATTACKS IN DEBATE

DR. WATSON: I don't know how we can consider building a soccer stadium in the middle of Underberg when it's clear that for decades the developers who want to do this have been dipping into the county treasury through kickbacks!

(Dr. Watson takes his seat)

MR. HOLMES: Mr. Chairman!

(Mr. Holmes rises)

CHAIR: Mr. Holmes, do you wish to speak in favor of the motion?

MR. HOLMES: Yes, I do. Mr. Chairman, I believe there is strong evidence to the contrary of what my colleague is saying. I direct you to the budget documents presented here today, which indicate that these developers are receiving no more income from our county government than any other contractor working on projects of the same size.

fallacies that the opponent seems to have used in coming to an opinion. Calling an opponent names, making sarcastic remarks, or otherwise insulting the opponent are all out of order. In addition, members must stay away from accusations that another person is lying or deliberately distorting the truth.

- **SPEAK TO THE CHAIR.** The participants in a debate do not address one another directly. The formal practice of having opponents speak to the presiding officer automatically elevates the discourse and eliminates the temptation to demean an opponent. Even questions are directed to the chair: "Mr. Chairman, would my colleague share with us where he obtained his information?" Some smaller organizations dispense with this level of formal discourse, but it does establish a level of decorum that can be beneficial when even a small assembly (such as a board) engages in a great deal of spirited debate.

MOTIONS THAT ARE NOT DEBATABLE

Most motions are open to debate, but a few are not, generally because they involve issues or procedures that require immediate attention or because they are motions reserved for decisions by the chair. Here is the short list of nondebatable motions:

- **MOTION TO ADJOURN.** A motion to adjourn is decided by a simple majority vote.

- **MOTION TO CLOSE THE DEBATE.** This motion passes with a two-thirds majority once the limits of the debate have been reached.

- **MOTION TO LIMIT THE DEBATE OR EXTEND THE LIMITS OF THE DEBATE.** *Robert's Rules of Order* doesn't express much fondness for debating about debating. Once a motion is on the floor to extend the usual limits of the debate, a two-thirds majority
can pass that motion without further discussion.

- **MOTION FOR DIVISION OF THE ASSEMBLY.** If a single member calls for a vote that requires members to rise and divide into groups based on their "aye" or "no" notes, the assembly must comply.

- **CALL FOR THE QUESTION (OR PREVIOUS QUESTION).** A motion to call for the question stops the debate immediately. (American organizations tend to call for the question, whereas strict parliamentary language would have an assembly's members calling for the previous question.)

- **MOTION TO RECESS.** This motion usually requires immediate action, so debate is neither required nor indicated.

- **MOTION TO SUSPEND THE RULES OF ORDER.** As noted in chapter 3, sometimes suspension of the rules allows business to be conducted more efficiently by forestalling lengthy debate or other long-winded discourse. Usually, the suspension pertains to a single motion, and the rules are reinstated for the next order of business. A two-thirds majority passes a motion to suspend the rules, and no debate is required (this is not surprising since debate is often exactly what the suspension is intended to avoid).

- **MOTION TO SUSPEND THE STANDING RULES OF A CONVENTION.** A simple majority can choose to suspend the rules for a large assembly or special meeting without putting the assembled delegates through a debate.

- **MOTIONS RELATED TO VOTING.** A motion by a member to use a specific kind of voting method—for example, polling the members individually or using a written ballot—does not require debate. There are often clear reasons for doing something other than having members raise their hands or vote by voice. The right to call for a different method of voting when there is a good reason to do so is a right that belongs to every member of the assembly.

Limiting or Extending Debate

Robert's Rules propose no official limits on the duration of a debate, as long as there are members who have not yet spoken twice in one day. Each speaker must limit his or her argument to 10 minutes (or to whatever time limit the members' organization has established in its bylaws), but an assembly with many members who wish to speak can still find itself entangled in a protracted debate for hours or even days.

An organization may choose to set limits for all debates, or it may decide to **LIMIT THE DEBATE** on a specific contentious motion. The clock can also limit the debate (for example, a member can move that the debate end at a specific time or that there be no more than two hours of debate on an issue).

Just as debate can be limited, it also can be extended, and within the same motion. In this way, a member may move that the debate end at 5 p.m. but also that each member be allowed to speak for up to 15 minutes instead of the usual 10.

LIMITING DEBATE

MR. HOLMES: I move to limit debate.

CHAIR: How will debate be limited, Mr. Holmes?

MR. HOLMES: I move that each person speak for two minutes and that each person have the option of speaking three times during the debate.

MRS. WHITE: Second!

CHAIR: A motion has been made and seconded that we limit debate in the following manner: Each person will speak for two minutes, and each person may speak up to three times during the debate. All those in favor . . .

As explained earlier in this chapter, a motion to limit or extend the limits of debate cannot be debated in itself. Once the motion is made and seconded, the assembly moves directly to a vote on the proposed limits.

Closing the Debate

When a debate has come to a natural conclusion, reached the limits set for it, or simply gone on as long as the assembly deems necessary, the rules require a motion to close the debate. A **CALL FOR THE QUESTION** stops debate on the main motion. This subsidiary motion can also be used to stop a debate that has become acrimonious.

Calling for the question is not a sure-fire way to bring the debate to a close, however: A two-thirds vote is required to end the debate, so if more than one third of the members want to continue, they can defeat this motion.

CALLING FOR THE QUESTION

MRS. SMITH: . . . and I believe that the lack of popularity of our soccer team to date makes it clear that we should not support construction of a soccer stadium, one that will probably never draw an audience of any size likely to make the expenditure worthwhile.

(Mrs. Smith takes her seat)

MR. HOLMES: Mr. Chairman, I call for the question.

MR. RUSSELL: Second!

CHAIR: The question has been called, so debate must stop for a vote. A two-thirds majority is required to call for the question. All those in favor of calling for the question, raise your hands.

(Members in favor raise their hands)

CHAIR: All those opposed, raise your hands.

(Members opposed raise their hands)

CHAIR: There are not enough votes in favor of calling for the question, so the debate will continue.

MRS. WHITE: Mr. Chairman!

(Mrs. White rises)

CHAIR: Mrs. White, do you wish to speak in favor of the soccer stadium?

MRS. WHITE: I do.

CHAIR: Proceed.

(The debate continues)

It's a common belief among members of boards and other governing bodies that simply crying out "Question!" in the middle of a debate will bring the debate to an instant close. *Robert's Rules of Order* does not say this; in fact, the truth is quite the opposite. A member who calls out before being recognized by the chair is always out of order. No one may use this method to force a speaker to stop debating. Doing so would not only disrupt the proceedings, but also demonstrate the shouter's lack of respect for another member's freedom of speech and for all speakers' protected rights within the rules of order. If you should ever become the target of such a disruption, don't let yourself be intimidated by it. Show the shouting member this paragraph, and instruct your misinformed colleague to refrain from further outbursts.

CHAPTER FIVE

AMENDMENTS
Refining the Decision

Once debate begins on a main motion, the assembly may find that the motion needs to be worded differently so that it reflects exactly what the organization wants to accomplish. Parliamentary procedure makes it fairly simple to change the language of a motion before it comes to a vote.

A change to a motion is called an amendment, and a vote by the assembly is required before the change can be made. In smaller organizations, an amendment may simply come up in the course of discussing the motion, and the group may be able to build a level of consensus before the motion is brought to a vote. In larger assemblies, an amendment may require as much debate as the motion itself.

PRESENTING AN AMENDMENT

Suppose you're a member of the board of what we'll call the National Award of Literary Excellence Foundation. You and your colleagues are planning to add a new award to your roster this year, but you're struggling over the categories for it.

The motion on the floor reads as follows: "The National Award of Literary Excellence Foundation will establish the Self-Published Book Award in the fiction and nonfiction categories."

You think these two broad categories are too limiting. You'd like to break the fiction category into several genres: romance, mystery, fantasy, science fiction, and general fiction. How do you proceed?

1. Write out exactly how the amended motion should read: "The National Award of Literary Excellence Foundation will establish the Self-Published Book Award in the romance, mystery, fantasy, science fiction, general fiction, and nonfiction categories."

2. During debate on the motion, ask to be recognized by the chair.

3. Present the amendment exactly as you have written it. Say, "I move that we amend the motion on the floor to read, 'The National Award of Literary Excellence Foundation will establish the Self-Published Book Award in the romance, mystery, fantasy, science fiction, general fiction, and nonfiction categories.'" Alternatively, you may say, "I move to replace the word 'fiction' in the main motion and insert the following words in its place: 'romance, mystery, fantasy, science fiction, general fiction.'"

4. Because the National Award of Literary Excellence Foundation, like many other organizations, requires amendments to be submitted in written form, the chair asks you for the paper on which you've written your amendment, and you give it to the chair.

5. The chair reads your amendment back to the assembly and asks for a second, if one has not already been offered.

6. With a motion and a second, debate begins on your amendment, just as it would for any other type of debatable motion.

7. Debate closes, and your amendment comes up for a vote. Your amendment is approved, but its passage only signifies that the new wording can be added to the main motion. The main motion still requires its own vote.

8. Debate closes on the main motion, and the vote is taken on the main motion as amended. The main motion passes, which means that the assembly has decided to do what you amended the motion to do.

TYPES OF AMENDMENTS

This section describes three basic types of amendments: changes to particular words (as in the procedure just outlined), changes to particular paragraphs, and changes to an amendment itself.

Word Changes

As we've seen, it's fairly simple to propose that particular words in a motion be replaced with other words. When you are recognized by the chair, say, "I move that we replace [*one or more words*] with [*one or more words*]."

INSERTION

If you want to *insert* words into a main motion, be very specific. Let's return to the meeting of our National Award of Literary Excellence Foundation and start with a main motion: "The National Award of Literary Excellence Foundation will establish the Self-Published Book Award in the fiction and nonfiction categories."

This time you would like to amend the motion to include narrative nonfiction, journalistic nonfiction, and memoir nonfiction as separate categories. Write your proposed amendment out on paper, and when the chair recognizes you, say, "I move that we insert the words 'narrative, journalistic, and memoir' before the word 'nonfiction' in the main motion." Your proposed amendment is an amendment to insert words.

After the chair has read your motion to the assembly, debate focuses entirely on inserting your proposed changes into the main motion. No additional amendments can be proposed until the amendment on the floor has come to a vote. This is because each new proposal for a change requires a new motion to amend the main motion.

STRIKEOUT

To *remove* a word from a main motion, you will use the same general procedure, but your motion will be slightly different.

Suppose you feel that the awards should be only for nonfiction. In proposing this amendment to the chair, you would say, "I move that we strike out the words 'fiction and' from the main motion." Your proposed amendment is an amendment to strike out words.

AMENDMENT TO INSERT WORDS

The members of the board of the National Award of Literary Excellence Foundation continue their discussion on the motion to create the foundation's Self-Published Book Award.

MR. GREEN: Madam Chairman!

(Mr. Green rises)

CHAIR: Mr. Green.

MR. GREEN: I move that we insert the words, "narrative, journalistic, and memoir" before the word "nonfiction" in the main motion.

(Mr. Green takes his seat)

MRS. BLUE: Second!

CHAIR: It has been moved and seconded that we insert the words "narrative, journalistic, and memoir" before the word "nonfiction" in the main motion. If the amendment is adopted, the motion will read as follows: "The National Award of Literary Excellence Foundation will establish the Self-Published Book Award in the fiction and narrative, journalistic, and memoir nonfiction categories." The question is on inserting the words "narrative, journalistic, and memoir" into the current motion. You may now debate the question.

STRIKEOUT WITH INSERTION

In a single motion, you can propose to remove some words and add others. Not only does this save time, since every amendment requires its own debate and its own vote, it may also clear up ambiguities quickly, especially if the debate centers on the wording of the original motion. Your proposed amendment is an amendment to strike out and insert words.

AMENDMENT TO STRIKE OUT AND INSERT WORDS

MR. GREEN: Madam Chairman!

(Mr. Green rises)

CHAIR: Mr. Green.

MR. GREEN: I move that we strike out the words "fiction and" and insert the words "narrative, journalistic, and memoir" before the word "nonfiction" in the main motion.

(Mr. Green takes his seat)

MRS. BLUE: Second!

CHAIR: It has been moved and seconded that we strike out the words "fiction and" and insert the words "narrative, journalistic, and memoir" before the word "nonfiction" in the main motion. If the amendment is adopted, the motion will read as follows: "The National Award of Literary Excellence Foundation will establish the Self-Published Book Award in the narrative, journalistic, and memoir nonfiction categories." The question is on striking out the words "fiction and" and inserting the words "narrative, journalistic, and memoir" into the current motion. You may now debate the question.

Paragraph Changes

In assemblies where very long documents come up for changes may affect entire paragraphs and sections rather than individual words and phrases. The methods for making amendments to entire paragraphs and sections are similar to those used for making changes to words, but here there is another type of amendment as well: the amendment to **SUBSTITUTE**.

INSERTION OR ADDITION OF A
PARAGRAPH, SECTION, OR ARTICLE

Just as you would do if you were proposing to insert or add a few words, write out the paragraph that you would like to see inserted into the document under discussion (in this example, a set of bylaws). When you address the chair, say, "I move that we insert this paragraph before paragraph 26 of the bylaws in the main motion," and then read your proposed paragraph aloud. Once you have a second, the chair will read your proposed paragraph aloud once more before opening the floor to debate about your motion.

STRIKEOUT OF A PARAGRAPH,
SECTION, OR ARTICLE

Here, you will read aloud the paragraph that you want to see struck from the document under discussion (or you can simply call the paragraph by its number, if it has one). When your proposed amendment is seconded, the chair will read aloud (or call by its number) the paragraph you propose to have removed and will then open the floor to debate.

SUBSTITUTION OF A PARAGRAPH,
SECTION, OR ARTICLE

Let's say that instead of simply adding or deleting a paragraph or section, you would like to replace an existing paragraph, or even an entire motion, with a completely different paragraph. Suppose, for example, it became clear during debate that the current motion needs more thought and a different thrust from what was originally proposed. In view of this development, you want to change the original motion ("The National Award of Literary Excellence Foundation will establish the Self-Published Book Award in the fiction and nonfiction categories") to something

AMENDMENT TO SUBSTITUTE

MR. GREEN: Madam Chairman!

(Mr. Green rises)

CHAIR: Mr. Green.

MR. GREEN: I move to substitute for the current pending motion the following amendment: "The National Award of Literary Excellence Foundation will form a committee to research
the different genres now included in fiction and nonfiction and will make recommendations to the main assembly in two months' time."

(Mr. Green takes his seat)

MRS. BLUE: Second!

CHAIR: A motion has been made and seconded that we substitute for the current pending motion the following: "The National Award of Literary Excellence Foundation will form a committee to research the different genres now included in fiction and nonfiction and will make recommendations to the main assembly in two months' time." Is there debate?

(The assembly debates Mr. Green's motion to substitute)

CHAIR: The question is on the motion to substitute the current pending motion with the following amendment: "The National Award of Literary Excellence Foundation will form a committee to research the different genres now included in fiction and nonfiction and will make recommendations to the main assembly in two months' time." The question is this: Shall we substitute this amendment for the current pending motion? All those in favor, raise your hands.

(Members in favor raise hands)

CHAIR: All those opposed, raise your hands.

> *(Members opposed raise hands)*
>
> **CHAIR:** Those in favor have it. The motion is passed. We will now debate the motion as amended: "The National Award of Literary Excellence Foundation will form a committee to research the different genres now included in fiction and non-fiction and will make recommendations to the main assembly in two months' time."

quite different: "The National Award of Literary Excellence Foundation will form a committee to research the different genres now included in fiction and nonfiction and will make recommendations to the main assembly in two months' time." Your proposed amendment is an amendment to substitute. It entails a significant departure from the original motion, and so a special kind of amendment is needed to move it forward. Any debate will be on the motion to substitute, not on the main motion.

Amendments to Amendments

Let's say that your motion to amend the main motion is now on the floor and under debate, but the assembly begins to see that another set of changes will be required to focus the meaning of the amended text as sharply as possible. At this point, you have two options that will help you achieve the desired level of clarity. The first is complex, and the second is fairly simple:

1. **PROPOSE A SECONDARY AMENDMENT.** You can amend your amendment by going through the same process of strikeouts, insertions, and replacements that you followed to create it originally. When these changes have been proposed and approved before the assembly votes on the

original amendment, they are known as amendments of the second degree, or amendments to amendments. *Robert's Rules of Order* provides a complex hierarchy of methods for getting secondary amendments to track all the way back to the main motion.

2. **GO BACK TO SQUARE ONE.** To take the much easier route, the assembly can vote the main motion down. The main motion is then rewritten, and a member of the assembly proposes the rewritten main motion with its revised wording and new meaning. This option takes much less time than plodding through a series of amendments, and it keeps the group from getting bogged down in layers of parliamentary procedure.

SPECIAL RULES FOR AMENDMENTS

The Germaneness Rule

Some legislative bodies, boards, and other groups that deal with controversial issues attempt to tack less popular motions onto motions that will pass easily in hopes of hiding a controversial decision under one that is likely to have wide support. In 2009, for example, the US House of Representatives passed a bill to reform the credit card industry and added a one-sentence amendment repealing the ban on carrying guns into the National Park Service's land and wildlife refuges. Obviously, there is no connection between the credit card industry and the presence of guns in the national parks. In other words, the right to bear arms in a wildlife refuge is not germane to the credit card industry.

Congress goes its own way, but *Robert's Rules of Order* expressly disallows such use of amendments. Let's look again at this motion: "The National Award of Literary Excellence Foundation will form a committee to research the different genres now included in fiction and nonfiction and will make recommendations to the main assembly in two months' time." In keeping with the germaneness rule, the voting members of the foundation cannot amend the motion unless the amendment has to do with the genres included in the fiction and nonfiction categories or with the timing of the proposed committee's recommendations. They cannot amend the motion by adding, for instance, "The National Award of Literary Excellence Foundation will also examine the use of bank accounts in the Cayman Islands as a way to protect and increase the foundation's cash reserves." Financial matters are important, of course, but they need motions of their own.

The "Settled" ("No Takebacks") Rule

Under the rules of parliamentary procedure, once an amendment has passed, it is considered to be settled. This means that a member of the assembly who is dissatisfied with the outcome cannot move to reopen discussion of the amendment or introduce further amendments that change the language of the amendment on which the assembly has just voted.

In some cases, as we have seen, a substitution amendment can alter a motion by replacing a chunk of language that includes the few words to which a member objects. Even then, however, the assembly must vote on the substitution amendment—and it's up to the assembly to vote down anything that looks like a deliberate obstruction to progress. Robert's Rules are highly detailed, but they also lean toward expediency by giving organizations the procedures they need to prevent members from becoming enmeshed in conflicts.

CHAPTER SIX

POSTPONEMENT AND REFERRAL
Saving a Motion for Later

Robert's Rules include simple procedures for setting aside one piece of business to take up one that's more urgent.

MOVING TO POSTPONE A MOTION

The move to postpone a motion offers flexibility and allows more time to reach a decision. A motion cannot be postponed indefinitely, however, unless the assembly takes a specific vote to do so (**see chapter 3**). The implication here, of course, is that a motion to postpone can be debated, especially if there are strong feelings about reaching a decision on the motion during the current meeting.

In most cases, the postponed motion (now called an open motion) will be taken up again later in the current meeting after the assembly dispenses with more urgent business. If no time remains to address the open motion, it can be postponed until the next meeting. The postponed motion will come up on the agenda for that meeting after unfinished business.

MOTION TO POSTPONE

The members of the board of the National Award of Literary Excellence Foundation, continuing their meeting, move on to the next agenda item.

CHAIR: At this time we need to deal with an urgent matter regarding a budget allocation. Is there a motion to postpone discussion of the pending motion?

MR. GREEN: I move to postpone the pending motion until our next meeting on March 25.

MRS. BLUE: Second!

CHAIR: A motion has been made and seconded to postpone the pending motion until March 25. Does anyone wish to debate?

(Silence)

CHAIR: Very well. I put the question to a vote. The question is whether to postpone the pending motion to the next meeting on March 25. All those in favor, signify by saying, "Aye."

MEMBERS IN FAVOR: Aye.

CHAIR: All those opposed, signify by saying, "No."

(Silence)

CHAIR: The ayes have it. The motion to postpone is passed.

MOVING TO COMMIT (REFER) A MOTION

Sometimes the assembly agrees that a motion is not ready for a decision at the current meeting because it requires more study than the assembly can undertake. In this case, the assembly can

COMMIT (refer) the motion to a committee whose members will look into it more thoroughly.

Committees are the workhorses of any organization. They examine issues and determine what the next steps should be or whether any action should be taken at all.

There are two types of committees:

- **STANDING COMMITTEES.** These committees are always active. They may include an executive committee (made up of the organization's officers); a budget or finance committee; a fundraising (or development) committee, if the organization is a nonprofit; a nominating committee, for putting forward the names of new officers and board members; a marketing committee; and a strategic planning committee. The number and types of the standing committees are typically specified in the organization's bylaws (**see chapter 7**).

- **AD HOC COMMITTEES.** These committees are formed on an as-needed basis. They take on special projects and short-term tasks, such as managing a capital campaign or amending and updating bylaws.

The procedure for referring an issue to either type of committee is simple. In the case of a standing committee, a member says, for example, "I move that the motion be referred to the Finance Committee for further study and that the committee report to the assembly two meetings from now." Note that this motion sets a specific date on which the committee will report back to the assembly.

When a motion is referred to an ad hoc committee, the mover should specify the committee's structure and leadership.

FORMING AN AD HOC COMMITTEE

MR. GREEN: Mr. Chairman!

CHAIR: Mr. Green.

(Mr. Green rises)

MR. GREEN: I move that we create a capital campaign committee of 10 people and that the chair of the committee be Mr. Fielding. Mr. Fielding will recruit the nine members of the committee by using his connections within and outside of this board.

(Mr. Green takes his seat)

MRS. BLUE: Second!

After the motion to refer to an ad hoc committee has been seconded, the procedure is the same as for any other kind of motion: The chair opens the floor to debate and then brings the motion to a vote.

CHAPTER SEVEN

DEMOCRATIC PROCESS
Knowing, Following, and Using the Rules

The first thing to be said about rules is that any organization must follow the laws of the state and country in which it operates. In addition, an incorporated organization will have a set of rules that govern its behavior. (If you are involved with a nonprofit organization, an unincorporated business, a social group, or a fraternal organization, it probably does not have a corporate charter.)

Apart from state and federal laws or corporate charters, every organization that uses a democratic process to make decisions will need rules to guide those decisions. The organization also needs rules to govern its operations and keep its activities aligned with the reasons for its existence.

TYPES OF RULES

Not only are there a number of different kinds of rules, there is also an established hierarchy to be followed when one rule seems to contradict another. This section discusses bylaws, rules of order, standing rules, and rules derived from customs.

Bylaws

For its decision-making operations, an organization requires its own set of rules that determine who is in charge, what actions are right and appropriate, and what kinds of activities the organization will undertake. These rules are known as bylaws. If you are a new member and will be involved in making decisions, you should receive a copy of the bylaws and any other rules observed by your organization. (If no one offers you a copy, ask the secretary for one.) This information may seem arcane and even dull, but it's your responsibility as a decision maker to know what the rules are and what is expected of you.

An organization's bylaws describe its purpose—the reasons it exists—and provide rules for the election of officers and the responsibilities of each officer. Bylaws also eliminate any ambiguities about what the organization expects from its officers, assembly, members, and employees (if it has any).

Bylaws usually provide instruction on these topics:

- The process for selecting members
- Required qualifications of members of the assembly
- The names and responsibilities of standing committees
- The frequency and duration of meetings
- The number of members required for a quorum

- The titles of organizational officers and the responsibilities of each officer
- Term limits, if any, for board members and officers
- Procedures to be used during board meetings and other assemblies
- Methods for settling disputes among members
- How conflicts of interest are defined for board members and others involved in decision making and the procedures for working through such conflicts

Rules of Order

Rules of order are the rules of parliamentary procedure used by a decision-making body. *Robert's Rules of Order* is probably the rule-making foundation for most organizations, and an organization will say so in its bylaws if that is the case. An organization may also have rules of order specific to its own needs (for example, the US Congress has modified some aspects of parliamentary procedure to fit its own requirements).

Standing Rules

These rules usually cover administrative details that are not necessarily discussed in standard bylaws. For example, if an organization's business requires rules related to procedures that are relevant only to that kind of business, then the organization may have another set of highly specific rules in addition to its bylaws. Or maybe the organization holds elaborate swearing-in ceremonies for new members and has a set of rules intended to ensure that these ceremonies are performed the same way every time. Or perhaps it's a standing rule that the secretary tracks the birthdays of all members and provides a cake for the assembly when a member's birthday falls on the day of a meeting. This is not the kind of rule that needs to be spelled out in the bylaws, but it may still be written down so each new secretary understands that this is part of the secretary's job.

Rules Derived from Customs

Some things may be done at meetings simply because they have always been done. For example, an organization may always close its meetings with a period when members are invited to share personal information about events going on in their lives. It's a nice tradition, but the bylaws don't require it, so it's a custom. If an organization decides to drop a custom, it can do so with a simple majority vote.

ENFORCING AND SUSPENDING THE RULES

If you are well versed in your organization's bylaws and rules of order, you are in a strong position to respond appropriately when you notice someone breaking the rules during a meeting. *Robert's Rules of Order* provides several methods for taking corrective action.

Raising a Point of Order

When you see a motion or another piece of business going forward without attention to all the proper steps, it's your duty to interrupt the proceedings. Stand up and say, "Point of order!" You do not need to wait for the chair to recognize you, especially if you are calling the point on the chair's error. State your point immediately and sit down. The chair will then rule on whether your point is valid.

It's very important to call a point of order as soon as you see a misstep. For example, suppose a motion has passed with no call for opposing votes and the assembly has moved on to its next piece of business. If you wait to call your point of order until debate is in full swing on the current motion, you'll be too late. The vote has already been taken on the previous motion, and there's no going back without a motion to reconsider that vote (**see chapter 3**).

Making an Appeal

If the chair makes a ruling with which you disagree, you may appeal that ruling to the assembly—not to the chair. The appeal gives the assembly a way to overrule the chair when a ruling does not follow the organization's bylaws, rules of order, or standing rules.

To make an appeal, you must act when the perceived infraction takes place. Stand and say, "I appeal from the decision of the chair." You do not need to be recognized by the chair, but another member must second your appeal so it can go forward.

The question of whether your appeal can be opened for debate is somewhat complicated. In brief, an appeal cannot be debated in the following circumstances:

- It has to do with the chair's breach of the rules of decorum (**see chapter 2**).

- It concerns the priority of the assembly's business, which should have been established at the start of the meeting (**see chapter 2**).

- It is made on a question or motion that is already ineligible for debate (**see chapter 3**).

Otherwise, the assembly can engage in debate about your appeal. Each member can speak only once, however—each member, that is, except the chair, who may state his or her case at the beginning of the debate and again at the end. At the close of the debate, the chair asks, "Shall the decision of the chair be sustained?" A majority of "no" votes means that your appeal has won. If there is a tie, the chair's decision is sustained, and you have lost your appeal.

POINT OF ORDER AND APPEAL

The members of the board of directors of the Girl Scouts of Pennington County continue their monthly meeting.

PRESIDENT: The motion has been amended that the Girl Scouts of Pennington County will combine troops 266 and 494 into one troop and that the new troop will meet monthly in a location to be determined, one that is an equal distance from each troop's elementary school.

MRS. O'HARA: Point of order!

(Mrs. O'Hara rises)

PRESIDENT: The member will state her point of order.

MRS. O'HARA: Our bylaws state that troops choose a meeting location not more than ten miles from the public school that the majority of the troop members attend. The amendment will put the meeting place outside that boundary for both troops.

PRESIDENT: The chair rules that the point of order is well taken. The bylaws do call for short traveling distances. That said, our bylaws require troops of at least 10 members each, and there are not enough scouts in either of these two troops to constitute a full troop. The amendment offers an appropriate compromise.

MRS. O'HARA: I appeal from the decision of the chair.

(Mrs. O'Hara takes her seat)

DR. JENKINS: Second!

PRESIDENT: The decision of the chair is appealed from. The chair's ruling was that the amendment proposing that the two troops choose a meeting place equidistant from their respective school locations was appropriate in this case. The question is this: Shall the decision of the chair be sustained? I will speak first, as the rules allow. Although our bylaws require that we choose meeting locations that are not more than 10 miles from each troop's central elementary school, choosing a location that is a little farther than 10 miles will allow us to continue to offer scouting opportunities to two small rural school districts that do not have enough members to qualify on their own.

MRS. O'HARA: Madam President!

(Mrs. O'Hara rises)

PRESIDENT: Mrs. O'Hara.

MRS. O'HARA: Making this change requires an amendment to our bylaws to allow troops to meet farther than 10 miles from their schools. We should table this motion and amendment and proceed to change the bylaws to make it allowable.

(Mrs. O'Hara takes her seat)

PRESIDENT: Who wishes to speak in favor of the decision?

MRS. SMITH: Madam President!

(Mrs. Smith rises)

(continued next page)

(continued from previous page)

PRESIDENT: Mrs. Smith.

MRS. SMITH: Postponing this decision means that these two troops will not meet at all until we make the decision. I am concerned that we will lose these children as a troop if we do not move quickly to combine the two troops. I also do not want these girls to leave scouting because their troops are not large enough to meet and carry on meaningful activities.

(Mrs. Smith takes her seat)

PRESIDENT: Are there others who wish to speak?

(The president pauses)

PRESIDENT: I will close with a rebuttal. Although there are rules in place that govern both the length of a parent's drive to a troop meeting and the size of each troop, there is also a rule that the welfare and involvement of young girls in scouting takes precedence. The question is this: Shall the decision of the chair be sustained? Those in favor of sustaining the chair's decision, signify by raising your hands.

(The president counts hands of those in favor)

PRESIDENT: Those opposed, signify by raising your hands.

(The president counts the hands of those opposed)

PRESIDENT: Those in favor have it. The decision of the chair is sustained. The motion has been amended that the Girl Scouts of Pennington County will combine troops 266 and 494 into one troop and that the new troop will meet monthly in a location to be determined, one that is an equal distance from each troop's elementary school.

Moving to Suspend the Rules

Making an appeal is not the only way to resolve a disagreement over a decision by the chair. Instead, a member may make a motion to suspend the rules in order to reach a single decision. A motion to suspend the rules can be used for something as basic as allowing one standing committee to report before another one, or something as complex as making an emergency budget allocation in circumstances that were not foreseen at the time of the annual meeting.

This motion has to be seconded, but it is not debatable. As a result, it is a far simpler process than making an appeal, which allows for debate and can halt progress—a frustrating situation when a beneficial outcome is hoped for.

Making a Parliamentary Inquiry

If you need to check a point of procedure with the chair, you have the option of interrupting the proceedings to make a **PARLIAMENTARY INQUIRY**. This is not a motion, and so it does not require a second or a vote. You are simply asking a question so you can phrase a motion properly or determine how to proceed on an issue.

Keep in mind, however, that the chair's response to your question will not necessarily be correct. Therefore, you may want to make your inquiry before the meeting by consulting your organization's **PARLIAMENTARIAN**, if the chair has appointed one. He or she can be expected to have a thorough knowledge of the rules of order and can also answer your question during the meeting, if the chair is willing to defer to the parliamentarian when you make your inquiry.

SUSPENDING THE RULES

PRESIDENT: The motion has been amended that the Girl Scouts of Pennington County will combine troops 266 and 494 into one troop and that the new troop will meet monthly in a location to be determined, one that is an equal distance from each troop's elementary school.

MS. JONES: Madam President!

(Ms. Jones rises)

PRESIDENT: Ms. Jones.

MS. JONES: I move to suspend the rules so as to remove the restriction that the troops meet less than 10 miles from their central elementary school.

(Ms. Jones takes her seat)

MRS. ORWELL: Second!

PRESIDENT: It has been moved and seconded to suspend the rules so as to remove the restriction that the troops meet less than 10 miles from their central elementary school. All those in favor, say, "Aye."

MEMBERS: Aye.

PRESIDENT: All those opposed, say, "No."

MRS. O'HARA: No.

PRESIDENT: The ayes have it, and the rules are suspended for the purpose of the motion that the Girl Scouts of Pennington County will combine troops 266 and 494 into one troop and that the new troop will meet monthly in a location to be determined, one that is an equal distance from each troop's elementary school.

Invoking Disciplinary Measures

An organization's bylaws may make provisions for term limits. If so, those provisions will be helpful if an exit date has to be set for a difficult or dishonest member of the organization's assembly or board.

In the case of a board member, if no term limits are explicitly stated, the bylaws may include a clause stipulating that a board member remains on the board until a successor is elected. If so, the troublesome member can be removed with a simple two-thirds majority vote as long as a successor has already been approved by the board.

For organizations whose bylaws don't offer these options, *Robert's Rules of Order Newly Revised* includes an entire chapter on the disciplinary process; see the **Resources** section at the end of this book for information on how to obtain a copy of the book's authoritative eleventh edition.

DEMOCRATIC PROCESS

CHAPTER EIGHT

VOTING
Making Your Voice Heard

Voting, the most basic and necessary decision-making tool, involves a set of well-defined rules and concepts.

MAJORITIES, PLURALITIES, AND UNANIMOUS CONSENT

- **MAJORITY.** A majority is defined as more than 50 percent of the total votes cast by those members who are eligible to vote. For example, if candidate or motion A gets 49 percent of the vote and candidate or motion B gets 51 percent of the vote, then candidate or motion B wins. **ABSTENTIONS,** the term used in connection with people who abstain (refrain) from voting, are not counted as votes against a candidate or a motion.

- **PLURALITY.** A **PLURALITY** is possible when (1) there are more than two alternatives to be considered, (2) more votes are cast for one of the alternatives than for the others, and (3) the alternative with the most votes has won less than

50 percent of the total votes cast. For example, if candidate or motion A gets 22 percent of the vote, candidate or motion B gets 37 percent of the vote, and candidate or motion C gets 41 percent of the vote, then candidate or motion C has a plurality. According to Robert's Rules, however, a plurality is not a winning vote. A majority is required to carry a motion or win an election. If the vote has produced a plurality, multiple ballots may be required for the outcome to be determined.

- **TWO-THIRDS MAJORITY.** In some cases, the rules require two-thirds of the eligible voters to vote for a motion in order for it to pass. For example, two-thirds of the voters must vote in favor of suspending the rules (**see chapter 3**).

- **MAJORITY OF THE ENTIRE MEMBERSHIP.** This type of majority, most often required for amendments to an organization's constitution or bylaws, or for the rescinding of a previous vote, usually requires a longer balloting process so that all eligible members can participate in the vote, regardless of whether they are able to attend a specific meeting.

- **UNANIMOUS CONSENT.** Not every motion requires lengthy debate and a voting process in order to be approved. When there is no opposition to a particular motion, the group can opt to pass it by **UNANIMOUS CONSENT**. The chair can also use unanimous consent to settle simple procedural questions.

TYPES OF VOTES

- **VOICE VOTE.** This is the most common method of voting, used when a simple majority is required to approve a motion. Here, voting members say either "aye" or "no" when the chair calls on them to do so.

- **VOTE BY SHOW OF HANDS.** Used in small groups, the vote by show of hands allows the chair and the assembly to see that a majority has voted for or against a question. Counting is usually not required unless the vote appears very close.

- **STANDING VOTE.** A standing vote should be used when a two-thirds majority is required to pass a measure. Instead of saying "aye" or "no," the members of the assembly rise to signify their votes. If a voice vote has been taken and it remains unclear which side has the majority, the chair can

VOTING

APPROVAL BY DIVISION AND STANDING VOTE

The deliberations of the National Award of Literary Excellence Foundation continue.

CHAIR: The motion is as follows: "The National Award of Literary Excellence Foundation will form a committee to research the different genres now included in fiction and non-fiction and will make recommendations to the main assembly in two months' time." All those in favor, say, "Aye."

MEMBERS: Aye!

CHAIR: All those opposed, say, "No."

MEMBERS: No!

MRS. BLUE: Division!

CHAIR: Mrs. Blue has demanded a vote by division. All those in favor of the motion, please stand.

(Members in favor stand, and the chair counts them)

CHAIR: Be seated. All those opposed, please stand.

(Members in favor stand, and the chair counts them)

CHAIR: Be seated. The motion is passed. The National Award of Literary Excellence Foundation will form a committee to research the different genres now included in fiction and non-fiction and will make recommendations to the main assembly in two months' time.

follow the voice vote with a standing vote. After a voice vote, members have the right to question its outcome and demand a standing vote by calling out, "Division!"

APPROVAL BY COUNTED VOTE

CHAIR: The motion is as follows: "The National Award of Literary Excellence Foundation will form a committee to research the different genres now included in fiction and nonfiction and will make recommendations to the main assembly in two months' time." All those in favor, say, "Aye."

MEMBERS: Aye!

CHAIR: All those opposed, say, "No."

MEMBERS: No!

MR. WHITE: I move that the vote be counted!

CHAIR: Mr. White has demanded a counted vote. All those in favor of the motion, please stand and remain standing to be counted.

(Members in favor stand, and the chair counts them)

CHAIR: Be seated. All those opposed, please stand and remain standing to be counted.

(Members opposed stand, and the chair counts them)

CHAIR: Be seated. The vote is 14 for the measure and 12 against it. The affirmative has it, and the motion is adopted. The National Award of Literary Excellence Foundation will form a committee to research the different genres now included in fiction and nonfiction and will make recommendations to the main assembly in two months' time.

- **COUNTED VOTE.** If the vote is close, or if the number of hands raised or people standing is so unclear that it is impossible to tell which side won, the chair can repeat the vote and count the number of votes on each side of the motion.

SAMPLE TELLERS' REPORT

- **MOTION:** The Girl Scouts of Pennington County will combine troops 266 and 494 into one troop, and the new troop will meet monthly in a location to be determined, one that is an equal distance from each troop's elementary school.

- **NUMBER OF VOTES CAST:** 56

- **NUMBER OF VOTES NECESSARY FOR ADOPTION:** 29

- **VOTES IN FAVOR OF MOTION:** 35

- **VOTES OPPOSED TO MOTION:** 21

- **BALLOT VOTE.** When there is a good reason for members' votes to be kept secret, a ballot vote is the best option. In this situation, the chair nominates a chairman of tellers, along with as many other tellers as may be required to hand out, collect, and count the ballots. The tellers (including the chairman of tellers) and the chair are permitted to vote. To keep identities secret, the chair instructs all members to fold their ballots in the same way. Once the ballots are collected, the chair asks if all who wish to vote have done so and then announces, "Since all votes are cast, the polls are closed." The tellers count the ballots and submit a written report to the chair. The chairman of tellers reads the report to the assembly, and the chair repeats the tally from the report and announces whether the motion has been adopted or defeated.

NOMINATIONS AND ELECTIONS

Voting in organizations is not limited to the motions that members propose. Another major purpose of voting is the selection of an organization's officers and other leaders. Chapter 9 discusses the major types of roles in which members can serve. Here, we'll take a look at the nomination process for elective offices and other leadership positions.

A nomination formally proposes that someone fill an elective position in an organization. It presupposes that this person is willing and able to fill the position and that he or she is willing to run for election.

- **NOMINATION FROM THE FLOOR.** The name of a candidate for election can be proposed during a regular meeting held at the time when the organization normally elects its officers and other leaders. Any member may nominate someone by calling out the person's name. The nomination does not need a second. The chair hears the name and responds by saying, for example, "Mrs. Carpenter is nominated."

- **NOMINATION BY COMMITTEE.** Another option is for the organization to form a nominating committee that seeks candidates who are willing to become officers. Usually, the nominating committee searches the organization's own membership for people who are willing to become officers and who are seen as well suited to their potential roles. The nominating committee then presents a complete slate of candidates for approval by the organization's board of directors or governing body. Once the slate of candidates has been approved, the nominating committee may bring the entire slate to a vote at once, or the assembly may wish to elect the organization's officers individually. The organization's bylaws (**see chapter 7**) should establish the nominating committee as one of the organization's standing committees.

If more than one candidate has been nominated for an elective office, voting will probably take place by ballot. If only one person is running for an office, the chair can waive the need for a ballot and declare the nominee the winner. This is called **ACCLAMATION,** and it can be a big time-saver, especially if the organization has a nominating committee that presents a slate of candidates who are the only ones running for their respective offices.

If the ballot contains more than one candidate for any one office, then the person who receives the majority of the votes becomes the winner. When there are two or more candidates for a single office, the result may be a plurality. As explained

VOTING

earlier, a plurality is not enough to determine the winner. When one candidate has a plurality, the assembly may have to cast multiple ballots in order to produce a majority vote and decide the outcome.

The election results become final when the chair or the nominating committee notifies the winning candidate of the outcome and he or she consents to serve. If, for some reason, the person who was elected declines to serve, balloting must continue until someone else on the ballot receives a majority vote.

WHEN AND HOW DOES THE CHAIR VOTE?

In a small organization or committee, the chair is expected to vote.

In a general assembly—that is, when an entire board of directors meets, or when all the members of an organization come together—the chair maintains impartiality by not casting a vote in open session. If the chair's vote is needed to break a tie, however, or if the vote is by confidential ballot, then the chair can vote along with the rest of the voting members.

When the votes in favor of a motion exceed by only a single vote those that are opposed, the chair has the option of creating a tie by casting a vote against the motion. What this means is that the chair's vote will cause the motion to fail. The chair is not obliged to create a tie in this situation. Creating a tie is simply an option if the chair chooses to defeat the motion.

VOTING

CHAPTER NINE

LEADERSHIP
Rising in the Ranks

You have accepted the nomination for an official position in your organization, and you've been elected. Now that you're an officer, what do you need to know so you can fulfill the duties of your position at meetings according to Robert's Rules?

PRESIDENT

As the leader of your organization, you will preside over meetings regularly. If this is your first time as a president, you will serve yourself and the organization well by learning and memorizing the frequently used standard procedures that will come up in just about every meeting. Always remember that your role in the meeting is not to pontificate about your own views. You're there to conduct the business of the organization. Here are your principal responsibilities:

- **COMMUNICATING.** Communication before and during meetings will be key to your role. Let members know about each meeting's business by distributing an agenda before the meeting, along with any supporting documents that people will need as they make decisions.

- **KNOWING THE STANDARD ORDER OF BUSINESS.** As we've seen, there are standard steps and protocols for everything, including the order in which business is conducted at meetings. Make certain that you know what the important issues are, what business will be conducted at each meeting, and how to move business through swiftly and efficiently. When you move business through in a predictable manner, the members of your assembly know what to expect and how to prepare for their own responsibilities.

- **REPEATING YOURSELF.** Doing and saying the same things over and over again will become a big part of your life. You will find that you frequently repeat the wording of motions to make sure that all participants know exactly what they are voting on at each meeting. Be sure that the assembly understands the wording of amendments and the impact that amendments will have on the motions at hand. Robert's Rules, with all the repetition they require, are not just boring procedures. They facilitate the decisions that affect the way your organization conducts its business, decisions that in turn affect the lives of other people.

- **MANAGING.** You need to understand how to manage the steps of a meeting. That means learning what you and others need to know in order for members to carry out procedures such as bringing a motion to the floor, putting someone's name forward in nomination for an office, and bringing a motion to a vote. Again, everyone will thank you for keeping things moving.

- **MASTERING THE RULE BOOK.** You should be the most knowledgeable person in the room about Robert's Rules. That way, you can follow them yourself while also guiding others in how to conduct the business of the meeting. You'll be especially glad you've mastered the rules when you have to handle points of order, appeals, and other issues.

VICE PRESIDENT

As vice president, your main role is to take over if the president cannot attend a meeting. Be prepared for this eventuality so you can keep things moving smoothly at any meeting where you need to preside. If, for some reason, the president must step down, you will serve as president and handle all the president's tasks. That's why the responsibilities of the president's role apply to yours as well.

SECRETARY

As secretary, you'll find that meetings are not the only busy time for you. You'll be busy between meetings, too. It's your job to prepare documents, distribute information, manage the paperwork of the meeting, and help the president prepare by providing all necessary materials. Here are your principal responsibilities:

- **KEEPING MEMBERS INFORMED.** Always send out a notice to inform and remind members of the date, time, and place of the next meeting. It's also a good idea to send out a meeting calendar at the beginning of the fiscal or calendar year, but you'll still need to send a reminder as each meeting approaches.

- **PREPARING THE AGENDA.** Whether your organization uses a standard order of business or a less formal agenda, you and the president will need to collaborate before each meeting to put the agenda document together. It's advisable to distribute the agenda to members before the meeting and have copies available for every member who attends.

- **RECORDING MOTIONS.** If a member proposing a motion has not written it down on a paper that can be handed to the president, then you will be the one to write it out for the president. It's crucial to get the exact words from the mover, so after you've written the motion down, read it back to be sure you've got it right.

- **COUNTING VOTES.** The president may ask you to count votes on ballots or to serve as a second pair of eyes during standing votes.

- **PREPARING THE MINUTES.** This means creating a full record of what is decided in meetings, including the motions and amendments that were passed and defeated, among other official activities. You don't have to capture everything that is discussed or debated. Instead, your role is to record the results of the meeting's official business. Before the next meeting, send the last meeting's minutes out to the organization's members so they'll have an opportunity to read them and note any corrections that should be made.

- **HANDLING CORRECTIONS.** At the beginning of a meeting, if members request corrections to the minutes of the previous meeting, you will be the one to make those corrections. You don't need to redistribute the corrected minutes, however. Once they've been approved at the next meeting (along with any corrections), they become a matter of record.

TREASURER

As **TREASURER,** you are responsible for the fiscal management of the organization. On the basis of the organization's bylaws, you must manage the funds in your care, conducting no other transactions with this money except the official business of the organization. Because you have responsibilities that involve managing money, you are the organizational officer who will attract the closest scrutiny. Here are your principal responsibilities:

- **PREPARING AND PRESENTING INTERIM REPORTS.** You will provide a treasurer's report at each assembly meeting. Usually you will report the balance of funds on hand, account for the organization's cash flow since your last report, mention outstanding obligations, and report expected income.

- **PREPARING AND PRESENTING ANNUAL REPORTS.** Once a year, you will submit a financial report on the fiscal health of the organization. This report is usually prepared at the end of the fiscal year, wherever that falls in your organization's calendar. You will also work annually with outside auditors to conduct a complete review of the organization's accounts and financial statements. It's a good idea to prepare your end-of-year report and give it to the auditors before they begin their review process. If there is no evidence of fraud, you will present the audited report at the first meeting after the auditors have completed their work, and your report will be approved as "audited and found correct."

- **COLLECTING FUNDS.** It may be your job to collect dues and annual gifts from members of the assembly. If so, this role will be specified in your organization's bylaws.

COMMITTEE ROLES

As mentioned earlier, committees are the workhorses of an organization, so your participation in committee work is vital to the health and progress of your organization. The bulk of the organization's work gets done by committees. Final decisions about future directions are made at the level of the board, but the work required to execute those decisions is often carried out by committees.

Committees also take on motions referred to them by the assembly. When a committee has researched a motion, deliberated on the best course of action, and determined the most appropriate next step, a resolution is developed—that is, a statement of the action that the assembly should take on the motion. A resolution often looks like this:

> The Finance Committee wishes to report that it has considered the motion to provide funds for the Girl Scout Troops of Pennington County to plan a field trip to Custer State Park in the spring of 2017. The committee recommends the adoption of the following resolution: Resolved, that the Girl Scouts of Pennington County allocate $1,200 to provide a bus and overnight camping accommodations for a field trip

to Custer State Park in the spring of 2017, on a date to be determined.

The resolution will come up for a vote at the next meeting of the full assembly, when the committee chairperson brings the resolution to the assembly.

Committee Chairperson

If you agree to chair a committee, it's your job to call meetings of the committee and to preside over them, making sure that the committee's work is done in a timely manner. If the committee is small, you will take notes and distribute the minutes yourself. If it's a larger committee, you may appoint someone to complete this task for you. As a committee chair, you can make motions and debate on their behalf, and you can take a position against someone else's motion. When the work of the committee requires input from the full assembly, you will take the relevant information to the assembly, present a report, and state the committee's resolutions for action. Someone else at the meeting (often the chair) will present a motion that will lead to a decision about your committee's recommendations.

Committee Member

Committees rely on their members to attend meetings, participate in discussions, share their expertise, and perform the tasks assigned to them. As a committee member, you will be expected to arrive at each meeting prepared to report on progress or findings related to the tasks you agreed to undertake. A committee does not require a quorum at every meeting, but it does require its members to complete their assignments and participate fully in discussions. You play an important role in furthering the work of the organization, so honoring your commitments is paramount.

BOARD MEMBERS

Whether you serve on the large board of a major national corporation or the small board of a local nonprofit, you are there for a reason—to assist in governance by making decisions that are in the best interests of the organization and its constituents. How you do this will depend on the size of your board and the formality with which meetings are conducted. Your presiding officer will set the tone, and you may or may not find strict adherence to Robert's Rules as described in this book.

In many cases, the board of a small organization does not require its members to rise before the presiding officer will recognize them, and debate may be more along the lines of an informal discussion, in which the presiding officer freely participates. In the end, however, you will be required to vote on motions, and your participation as a board member will have more value if you attend meetings regularly.

At the very least, you will be needed at board meetings to help form a quorum. As you know, if there is no quorum, the board cannot make decisions, and the business of the organization comes to a standstill. This is one case in which it's absolutely true that a big part of success as a board member consists of showing up, especially when you serve on the board of a small organization. Take your responsibility seriously.

CONVENTION DELEGATES AND ALTERNATES

If you belong to the local chapter of a regional or national organization, your chapter may be required to send delegates to a convention, which is an assembly of chapter representatives from across the region or country. At the convention, goals will be set and rules will be made that affect the organization as a whole. Your organization's bylaws will set out specific duties for you as a delegate, which are likely to include the following:

- Registering as a delegate when you arrive at the convention

- Attending meetings at the convention

- Voting on motions presented at the convention in keeping with the instructions you've received from your chapter's leaders and assembly

- Presenting a report to your chapter when you return from the convention

Your chapter will also select alternate delegates. If you are an alternate delegate, you will also attend the convention, but you will have access only to the section of the hall reserved for alternates. If one of your chapter's official delegates has to drop out for some reason, you may be required to take that delegate's place. At the convention, you will register as an alternate delegate, but you will not vote unless you are called on to replace an official delegate and become an official delegate yourself.

APPENDIX

What to Say When, and How to Say It

WHEN YOU WANT TO DO THIS . . .	SAY THIS . . .
Make a motion	I move that . . .
Second a motion	Second!
Adjourn	I move to adjourn.
Amend a motion by inserting words	I move to amend the motion by inserting . . . [*say the words you want to insert, and indicate where they should go*].
Amend a motion by striking out words	I move to amend the motion by striking out the words . . . [*say the words you want to strike*].
Amend a motion by substituting	I move to amend the motion by substituting . . . [*say the words with which you want to replace the existing language*].
Abstain from voting	I abstain.
Commit or refer a motion to a committee that has not yet been formed	I move to refer the motion to a committee to be appointed by the chair.

Refer a motion to a standing committee	I move to refer the motion to the [name the committee].
Call for a counted vote	I move that the vote be counted.
Call for a standing (rising) vote	Division!
Call for debate to be closed	I move the previous question. or I call for the question.
Postpone the question to a certain time	I move that we postpone the question until [state the time and/or the date].
Limit debate	I propose that debate be limited to [state the number of minutes] per person.
Recess	I move that we recess until [state the time].
Suspend the rules	I move that we suspend the rules and . . . [state what you propose to take place with the rules suspended].
Demand an appeal	I appeal from the decision of the chair.
Make a parliamentary inquiry	Parliamentary inquiry, please.
Raise a point of order	Point of order! or I rise to a point of order. [When asked to raise the point], I raise the point of order that . . . [state the point of order].
Request information	I make a request for information.

GLOSSARY

ABSTENTION: A person who abstains (refrains) from voting on a motion; the act of abstaining.

ACCLAMATION: The chair's waiver of the requirement for a ballot when only one person is running for a specific office, and the chair's declaration that this single nominee is the winner.

ADJOURNMENT: The official closing of a meeting.

AGENDA: A changeable order of business for a specific meeting, often including the addition of activities that may not be directly related to the business of the organization.

AMENDMENT: A change in the language of a motion before it comes to a vote.

APPEAL: An assembly member's act of openly disagreeing with a ruling by the chair; to state such disagreement.

ASSEMBLY: A group of people who have come together to reach one or more decisions; the members in attendance at a meeting of the group.

BYLAWS: Rules that define why an organization exists and how it conducts official business.

CALL FOR THE QUESTION: A motion to end debate immediately.

CALL THE MEETING TO ORDER: To convene the meeting.

CHAIR: The person appointed or elected to lead a meeting, whether or not he or she is president of the organization; to serve as leader of a meeting.

(MOTION TO) COMMIT: A motion to send a motion to a committee for further study; also called "motion to refer."

DIVISION: A voting method in which members stand up to be counted.

FLOOR: Authorization to speak, as in "You have the floor;" the physical space in which motions are made and debated and voting takes place.

GERMANE: Having to do with the subject at hand.

LIMIT THE DEBATE: Set limits on the length of time each participant can speak and/or on the number of times each participant can speak during a given debate.

MAIN MOTION: A call to introduce a piece of business for the first time.

MAJORITY: More than half of the people in an assembly who are eligible to vote.

MINUTES: Notes that detail who was in attendance at the meeting, what motions were proposed, and what action was taken on each motion.

MOTION: An official proposal that members take action on a particular issue.

MOVER: The person who makes a motion.

OLD BUSINESS: Business already completed in previous meetings.

PARLIAMENTARIAN: A member of the assembly, recognized as the one most knowledgeable about parliamentary procedure, whom the chair has appointed to answer procedural questions during meetings, as well as on a more informal basis before and after meetings.

PARLIAMENTARY INQUIRY: A question about procedure in the course of a meeting.

PARLIAMENTARY PROCEDURE: The principles and procedures that govern the meetings of a legislature, especially the United Kingdom's supreme legislative body, known as Parliament.

PLURALITY: Those members of an assembly whose votes in favor of a single alternative outnumber the votes in favor of any other alternative when more than two are under consideration.

PRESIDENT: The officer who leads the organization.

PRESIDING OFFICER: The officer who conducts meetings of the assembly.

(MOVE OR CALL FOR THE) PREVIOUS QUESTION: A motion to end debate immediately.

PRIVILEGED MOTION: A motion that must be voted on before the meeting can continue.

QUORUM: The number of people required to be in attendance before a vote can be taken on any motion.

RECESS: A break in a meeting until a specific time.

(MOTION TO) REFER: A motion to send a motion to a committee for further study; also called "motion to commit."

REPORT: An overview of a committee's activity, of research, or of other information required for the assembly to come to a decision.

SECOND: A group member's immediate assent that the group should have permission to consider a motion just put forward by another member; to give such assent to another member's motion.

SECRETARY: The officer who prepares documents, takes minutes, creates the agenda, and performs other administrative tasks for the assembly.

SIMPLE MAJORITY: Exactly half the members of an assembly who are eligible to vote, plus one.

(ORDER TO) STAND AT EASE: The chair's instruction for the members of the assembly to remain in their seats while he or she confers with others until calling the meeting to order once again.

STANDARD ORDER OF BUSINESS: The established order in which procedures will be performed and business will be conducted at meetings.

STANDING COMMITTEE: A committee that must exist according to the bylaws of the organization.

SUBSIDIARY MOTION: A motion that affects the main motion currently on the floor.

SUBSTANTIVE BUSINESS: Any decisions that must be made during a meeting.

(AMENDMENT TO) SUBSTITUTE: An amendment that removes a set of words from a motion and replaces them with different words.

TABLE: To set a main motion aside until a later time.

TELLERS: People appointed by the chair to count votes for and against a motion and to create a report on the results.

TREASURER: The officer responsible for the financial health of the organization; responsibilities include preparing reports on cash flow, income, and expenses.

UNANIMOUS CONSENT: A means of passing a motion without holding a vote, if there is no opposition to the motion.

UNFINISHED BUSINESS: Business that was started at the last meeting and carried over to the current meeting.

VOTE: A poll of the assembly that is taken to reach a final decision on a motion; to state one's support for or opposition to the motion by means of such a poll.

YIELD: To finish speaking, or to give up the rest of one's allotted time to speak; not to be confused with the practice observed in the US Congress, for example, whereby one legislator can transfer ("yield") a portion of his or her allotted time to a legislative colleague.

RESOURCES

Given the copyright expiration of some earlier versions of *Robert's Rules of Order*, a variety of publishers, civic organizations, and other parties have brought the work out, in whole or in part, under a bewildering array of titles. If you want to use what is now recognized as the authoritative edition, here is the bibliographic information you will need:

> Robert, Henry M. III, Daniel H. Honemann, and
> Thomas J. Balch, with the assistance of Daniel E. Seabold
> and Shmuel Gerber. *Robert's Rules of Order Newly Revised*,
> 11th ed. Philadelphia: Da Capo Press, 2011.

The remainder of this section gives descriptive and background information about the eleven major editions of Robert's manual that have been published under three different titles between 1876 and 2011.

Pocket Manual of Rules of Order for Deliberative Assemblies

FIRST EDITION (1876, FEBRUARY). Robert's inaugural version of the book was loosely modeled on the rules followed in the US House of Representatives at the time of publication. The first edition had 176 pages, and 4,000 copies were printed.

SECOND EDITION (1876, JULY). Robert began adding details that were based on correspondence he had received from readers who had questions about specific parliamentary procedures. The second edition of the book had 192 pages, and the number of copies, at 141,000, amounted to more than 35 times the size of the first edition's print run.

THIRD EDITION (1893). Robert continued responding to readers' questions and studying the nuances of parliamentary procedure, as he would do throughout his life. The third edition had 218 pages and a print run of 375,000 copies, more than twice the number printed for the first and second editions combined.

Robert's Rules of Order Revised

FOURTH EDITION (1915). Revised and expanded by Henry M. Robert himself, this edition was the last major one that he completed before his death in 1923. It had 323 pages, and 570,000 copies were printed.

FIFTH EDITION (1943). This edition, like the sixth, was largely a reprint of the 1915 edition. It had 326 pages and a print run of 160,000 copies.

SIXTH EDITION (1951). Like the fifth edition, the sixth edition had 326 pages. But it had a print run of 675,000 copies, a prodigious total, perhaps accounted for by the fact that this was also the 75th anniversary edition of the book.

Robert's Rules of Order Newly Revised

SEVENTH EDITION (1970). When this edition appeared, it was hailed as the authoritative source on parliamentary procedure, and parliamentarians specified that it be named henceforth as the preferred reference in organizational bylaws. Enlarged to more than three times the size of the first edition and revised with clearer explanations, it had 594 pages, with 875,000 copies in print.

EIGHTH EDITION (1981). This edition was essentially a reissue of the seventh. Like that edition, it had 594 pages, but its print run, at 600,000 copies, was nearly 30 percent smaller.

NINTH EDITION (1990). With a redesign and a new, reader-friendlier typographic treatment, the ninth edition, expanded to 706 pages, also boasted the book's largest print run yet, at 1,050,000 copies.

TENTH EDITION (2000). If the ninth edition applied some welcome polish, the tenth went under the hood for a thorough editorial tune-up that imposed greater overall consistency and introduced simpler language. This edition had 704 pages, and 550,000 copies were printed.

ELEVENTH EDITION (2011). Seen as superseding all ten previous editions, this one significantly expands and updates many of the book's topics. It has 716 pages, and 500,000 copies have been printed to date.

Robert's Rules of Order Newly Revised in Brief

FIRST EDITION (2004) AND SECOND EDITION (2011). In both editions of this scaled-down pocket guide from Da Capo Press (also the publisher of the authoritative eleventh edition), the Robert's Rules Association provides novice assembly members with highlights they can use to get started as users of parliamentary procedure.

INDEX

C

D

F

G

I

R

S

CPSIA information can be obtained
at www.ICGtesting.com
Printed in the USA
LVHW010757180319
611007LV00013B/240

9 781623 156213